PUB W

I N

Northamptonshire

THIRTY CIRCULAR WALKS
AROUND NORTHAMPTONSHIRE INNS

Charles Whynne-Hammond

COUNTRYSIDE BOOKS
NEWBURY, BERKSHIRE

COUNTRYSIDE BOOKS
3 Catherine Road
Newbury, Berkshire

ISBN 1 85306 240 5

Cover illustration by Colin Doggett
Photographs by the author
Maps by Glenys Jones

Produced through MRM Associates Ltd., Reading
Typeset by Paragon Typesetters, Queensferry, Clwyd
Printed in England by J. W. Arrowsmith Ltd., Bristol

Contents

Area map shows location of the walks.

Introduction

Northamptonshire must be one of the most underrated – not to say least known – counties in England. It sits comfortably neither in East Anglia nor the Midlands, nor indeed in South-East England, yet it contains ingredients of each of those distinctive regions. It has the broad skies and wide horizons of East Anglia, the industrial townscapes and gritty Victorian atmosphere of the Midlands, and the rolling downlands and gentle, friendly meadows of the South-East. In short, it contains all the elements which produce good walking country. Add to these a wide selection of old village pubs and the assets are complete.

Topographically Northamptonshire can be sub-divided into two areas. The south-western half of the county – south of such villages as Welford and Brixworth – is geologically a continuation of the Cotswolds. It has broad limestone hills, deep valleys and beautiful honey-coloured stone villages. The north-eastern half of the county – from, say, Harrington and Great Cransley to the Lincolnshire border – is a district of flat plateaux, wide meadows and winding rivers. The landscape slopes gradually down towards the distant Wash and there are lakes and ponds rich in wildlife. The rock is still limestone, but here there is a greater iron content, making the villages greyer and darker in colour than those further south, but no less attractive.

This book includes walks from both these geographical areas, 17 in the former, 13 in the latter. A great variety of landscape is therefore covered: hill country and fenland, rough pasture and woodland, hedged water meadows and farmland. But more than this. The walks chosen have been carefully selected to provide the widest possible diversity of countryside. There are walks along canal towpaths and around lakes, walks through parklands landscaped by such famous designers as Capability Brown and Humphrey Repton, walks which follow the alignments of old railway lines, medieval roads and ancient drovers' ways. Some of the walks link villages of architectural and historic interest, others pass close to sites of archaeological importance: Celtic hill forts, ridge-and-furrow remains of strip cultivation, deserted villages of Saxon origin.

The lengths and ground conditions of the walks vary also. Some are short, easy strolls, suitable for a morning or an afternoon perambulation, others are proper walks, requiring time and some map-reading skills. The latter may cross some challenging country and involve short lengths of unclear footpath. There are even a few walks which have been especially chosen with young children and disabled people in mind. These employ trackways firm and flat enough for prams and wheelchairs, thus allowing the less mobile to share in the pleasures of the countryside.

The Ordnance Survey maps referred to in the text are from the 1:50 000 Landranger series, invaluable because they are on a scale useful to walkers, and because they include footpaths and bridleways.

The pubs in this book range from large, modernised food-orientated establishments to small, traditional inns where food is limited. All, however, are old, interesting, friendly and full of character, as well as being on the route of an enjoyable circular walk.

In general, pubs still keep to the established opening times. – termed 'normal' in the pub profiles: 11 or 11.30 am to 2.30 pm lunch-times, 6.30 or 7 pm to 11 pm evenings. These hours may be extended slightly on Saturdays and reduced slightly on Sundays. Those wishing to eat should aim for the reasonable 'sitting' times: 12 to 1.30 pm during lunchtimes and 7 to 10 pm during evenings. Variations in these times are given in the text, together with the telephone number of each pub so that prospective customers can check details beforehand. All the pubs mentioned in this book that have car parks allow patrons to leave their vehicles on the premises while they are walking. However, it is polite to inform the landlords before doing so.

Nowadays the choice of food offered by pubs is wide, bar snacks are also common. Only where specialities are offered, or where special diets are satisfied, are comments made in the text. Beers and real ales are also served with great choice at all the pubs in this book.

Walkers are welcomed at every establishment but courtesy is advised when wearing wet clothes and muddy boots. Large walking groups should telephone a pub before turning up since space is some-times limited in the bars. Eating one's own food in a pub which serves meals and snacks should not be attempted, except by prior arrangement. Most pubs now welcome dogs and children, especially if they are well behaved, but often only in certain bars or in the gardens. Again, it would be polite to check with the landlord before a visit.

I should like to thank all those pub proprietors who supplied me with valuable information regarding their establishments. I am also indebted to Glenys Jones for drawing the maps and illustrations for the book, and to Gwen Cassell who helped with the final draft. My brothers Alex and Peter, too, gave a certain moral support!

Charles Whynne-Hammond
Rothwell

Aynho
The Cartwright Arms

The name of this pub comes from the family that once owned the estate here and lived in the manor house opposite. After more than 300 years – the Cartwrights bought the estate in 1616 – the line died out in tragic circumstances, when, in 1954, Richard Cartwright and his only son, the heir, were killed in a car crash. So ended a dynasty which had sent members to the Peninsular War, to Waterloo and to the Crimea.

The Cartwright Arms is a handsome, stone-built hotel offering three bars and a separate restaurant. Inside there is a lot of wood and stone, preserving the character and age of the building, and open fires burn when the weather turns chilly. It is a free house serving a wide selection of real ales together with draught ciders and wines by the glass. There is always a large, and changing, menu both for main meals and bar snacks, but the rump steaks are well-advertised and are especially good.

The pub is open during normal times, although it is advisable to arrive for lunch early (shortly after midday) since the place can become very busy. Well-behaved dogs are allowed in and children are welcome.

Telephone: 01295 811111.

How to get there: The main road through Aynho, from Banbury (6 miles to the north-west) to Bicester (8 miles to the south-east) used to be the A41. It is now the B4100, due to the opening of the M40 motorway nearby. The Cartwright Arms faces this road, standing back a little, along a side road. Being at the top of the hill, there are good views to the west.

Parking: The pub courtyard, approached through an archway at the front, doubles as a car park. Otherwise, the village lanes being narrow and steep, it might be advisable to park along the roadside in the lane towards Charlton, close to the start of the walk.

Length of the walk: 4 miles. OS Landranger Map 151 Stratford-upon-Avon (GR: SP 515332).

The walk offers a pleasant expedition through countryside reminiscent of the Cotswolds. Not surprisingly, really, since the hills here are a continuation of the Cotswolds. They are made of the same rock – jurassic limestone – and have the same kinds of villages – with honey-coloured cottages, thatched roofs and well-tended gardens. The only difference to the Cotswolds proper are the crowds: this part of Northamptonshire does not have any!

The Walk

From the Cartwright Arms go down the main road to the right and take the turning to Charlton. Here on the right is a lovely row of cottages, old, yellow and mellowed with age. Just beyond, to the left and opposite a side road, you will see the signpost marking the footpath to Kings Sutton. There is a stone step stile here. Clamber over this and your walk has begun.

The path takes you along by the edge of a field, with the hedgerow on your right and a wide view to your left. And what a view. Rolling countryside, woodlands and low distant hills. The river Cherwell flows below you, and the Oxford canal, peaceful although sharing the valley with the new M40 motorway. Over a wooden stile the path continues across the next field and very soon the steeple of Kings Sutton church heaves into view directly ahead. The way is clear: around the edge of the next field, but continuing in the same direction, you find yourself descending. The path skirts to the right of a cluster of greenhouses and down into the hamlet of Walton Grounds.

Here is the plant breeding station of Twyford Seeds. No wonder there are so many greenhouses. Along the lane to the Twyford Seeds office (and visitors' car park) and then left, brings you to a concrete drive. Follow this and it soon becomes a country lane (past a couple

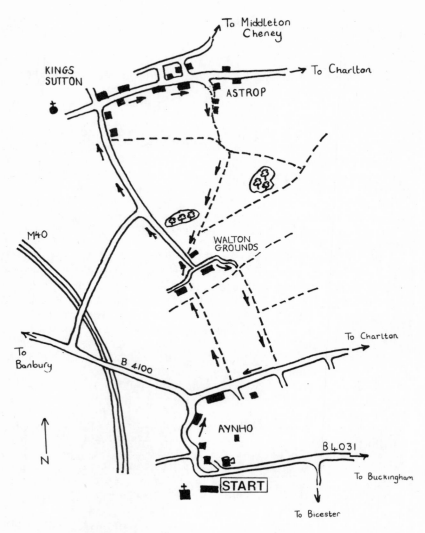

of red brick cottages on the right). From here to Kings Sutton is an easy walk. You simply follow the lane. It is not exactly busy. You will be lucky – or rather unlucky – if a single vehicle passes you, so you can enjoy the views without the worry of being run over. Within a mile you will reach Kings Sutton itself.

And what a lovely village it is. Overlooking the central green are numerous thatched cottages, a Jacobean manor house and – towering above all – the beautiful spire of the medieval church. Walking through the village, on the Charlton road, you pass a playing field on the left followed by the turning to Middleton Cheney. Immediately afterwards you turn right down an attractively shaded lane past some old stone cottages and farms. They are picturesque but look as though they have seen better times.

In fact, they have. This end of Kings Sutton is called Astrop. In the 18th century it was called Astrop Wells, for here was a spa resort of some renown. The health qualities of the springs and wells of the village were discovered and soon the rich and famous were heading this way, including Prime Minister's son Horace Walpole, the author. Nearby Astrop House – whose grounds were laid out by Capability Brown – became the centre for highly fashionable and aristocratic house parties. Sadly this popularity did not last. People started to go to Bath and Tunbridge Wells instead and – to hasten Astrop's decline – a dreadful fire in 1785 destroyed 40 houses. The spa resort became a ghost village.

At the end of the lane you bear to the right, avoiding a detached residence, and then left. From here a clear path leads ahead of you, running beside a hedgerow on the left. Beyond the stream, you can either make your way, by clear trackway, up to the skyline straight in front of you (where you will meet a bridleway and turn right) or you can bear half-right and cross the field diagonally. This will take you into the next field (be careful of the ditch) where you bear left to follow the hedgerow. You then cross the next two fields diagonally aiming, all the time, for a gap between two small woodlands. Whichever way you choose you will soon find yourself back at the Twyford Seeds establishment. Walk through the yard, between the animal sheds, and then right. A very clear track leads straight on.

Although uphill all the way the last mile of the walk is very pleasant. You find yourself on a wide grassy thoroughfare, with a good 20 ft between the hedgerows. At the edge of the Twyford Seed Company's land there is a gate and stile but still the trackway leads onwards. At the point where you meet the road (not far from where you started the walk) you will see – ahead of you – a road continuing in the same direction. It is called 'Portway'. And a 'portway' was an old name for a market road – a road that linked villages together to allow people to go from market to market. Turn right to follow the road back to the Cartwright Arms.

Chipping Warden
The Griffin

The original Griffin tavern was situated on the main road to Byfield, but it burned down in 1799 and its site is now occupied by a house called The Beeches. The present Griffin is a handsome stone building dating from the 18th century. Before it became a pub in the 1860s it was subdivided into three separate cottages. Today the roof is tiled but, before the last War, it was thatched. Even so, it is still an attractive structure, much enhanced by hanging baskets and creeper up the walls. The name is taken from the lords of Chipping Warden manor house during the 15th and 16th centuries. In those days the pub could well have been owned by those lords. Today, however, it is owned by Wolverhampton and Dudley Breweries and is, in consequence, a Banks's house.

Over recent years much renovation work, for the better, has gone on. There is a bar and a lounge (as well as a separate restaurant area) and the decoration is 'olde worlde' in the nicest sense. In the summer you can sit in the gardens at the back, in winter you can roast yourself at the open fires. The Griffin is open normal times and a full menu is offered both at lunchtimes and evenings. The food is good and reasonably priced.

Telephone: 01295 86230.

How to get there: Chipping Warden stands on the A361, 6 miles north of Banbury and 5 miles north of Junction 11 on the M40 motorway. It is very close to the county boundary with Oxfordshire. The Griffin is situated on the left of the Sulgrave road, on the edge of the village.

Parking: There is a pub car park. Vehicles can also be left on the roadside at certain places around the village.

Length of the walk: 2 miles. OS Landranger Map 151 Stratford-upon-Avon (GR: SP 500489).

This short walk would be suitable for those who wish to take very young children, or disabled people, out into the countryside. Prams and wheelchairs can be pushed, for the track is wide and firm underfoot. Although the return would have to be made along the same route as the outward journey the views would be different. For those without prams and wheelchairs there is a circular walk, and for a more strenuous outing there is an optional extension, involving a further 2 miles. But, whichever way you choose, do not rush. Savour the views, the wildlife and the architecture.

The route consists of a stroll through the landscaped parkland of Edgcote House and a wander through two most attractive settlements: rural England at its best. Throughout the walk you will see horses — there is a stud farm here — together with sheep and cattle grazing the fields. The landscape is nearly all pasture hereabouts, with trees dotted around at picturesque intervals.

The Walk

After turning right from the Griffin turn down the lane marked 'village only'. You will see the church over to your right and, to your left along the side of the lane, the limestone wall of the estate. The lodge gates into the estate (with the sign 'Private Road, Footpath only') you will see ahead, and these mark the start of your walk.

But look around the village first. Chipping Warden must be one of the loveliest villages in the county — ancient, stone-built cottages, many with thatched roofs, a medieval towered church, the base of an old stone cross. There are flowers everywhere for much of the year and tall trees cast their dappled shade.

Through the lodge gates you will find the trackway running ahead, slightly downhill. It is the old drive to Edgcote House. The surface is uneven but firm — a mixture of gravel and old metalling. It has seen better days (there are potholes and stony bumps) but with care a pram or wheelchair can be navigated along it. Where it crosses a small stream there is a wide bridge, and a little further, a farm gate. The former is flat and dry, the latter opens easily. The countryside either side is totally unspoilt. Beyond the landscaped pastures and trees the

13

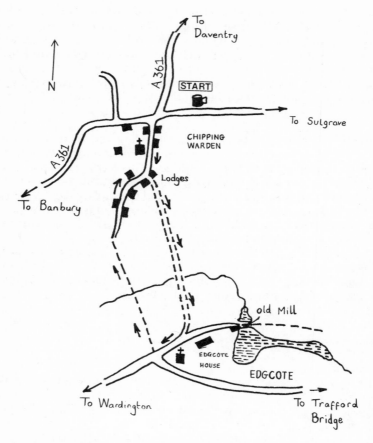

farmland opens out over the Northamptonshire Heights. Thenford Hill is on the skyline.

It is not far to the quiet and unspoilt hamlet of Edgcote. The House itself is a splendid classical mansion. To the right is the medieval church and down the lane which goes to the left is the mill. There the water spills out from the lake (which is behind the House and largely hidden by trees) and into an attractive pond. The old mill wheel has gone but the building is of some interest. It is hard to believe, in such a placid situation, that Edgcote has links historically with wars and battles. During the Wars of the Roses, in the 15th century, a great conflict took place just south of the hamlet. In that the Earl of Pembroke, in the service of King Edward IV, was killed. Two hundred years later, during England's other Civil War, Edgcote became a

14

Royalist stronghold. Charles I stayed here before the Battle of Edgehill (across the border in Warwickshire).

Those wishing to lengthen the walk can continue from the mill, over the bridge and along the trackway which bends round to the right. This will take them around the northern side of the lake to Trafford Bridge from where they can return to Edgcote by way of a minor country lane. Those with prams or wheelchairs can return to Chipping Warden by the drive taken earlier. This time, the journey is slightly uphill.

Others will return a different way. Passing the front of Edgcote House, and then the church, you will see a grassy track off to the right (opposite the lane from Trafford Bridge). This leads down the side of a field with the hedgerow on the right. In due course you come to the river, where you will find a bridge nestling under the trees. A pleasant spot this and you may wish to linger awhile enjoying the babble of the water and the rustle of wildlife. All around, the country is uncultivated so the wild flowers can be a joy to behold.

From here the path continues, now uphill. Soon it becomes a concrete lane and then a tarmac road. In no time you are back in Chipping Warden. And once again you can admire the cottages, gardens and trees as you return to the Griffin.

Sulgrave
The Star Inn

This lovely Grade II listed building is 300 years old and full of character. Inside, the oldest and most traditional part is the bar where there are flag-stone floors and low oak beams. Over recent years a separate dining room has been incorporated (for use by staying guests) and a function room has been added, but these have not detracted from the overall charm of the place.

It is a Hook Norton house and therefore serves Old Hooky and Hook Norton Best real ales. Scrumpy Jack cider is also available and various wines. But it is for its food that the Star Inn is justly famous. Each day the specialities are written up on a large blackboard – and scrumptious they are too. There are home-made soups, steak-and-kidney pies, unusual salads (like crab and avocado) and various continental dishes. Snacks include ploughman's lunches and 'double-decker' sandwiches (with meat or cheese or whatever in one layer and salad in the other). Vegetarians are catered for as well.

Whilst enjoying this fare you can admire the decor: a horned hare is mounted on the wall and 'George' the skeleton sits on a chair in the inglenook. There are also mementoes with an American flavour (since

Sulgrave Manor is nearly opposite, ancestral home of George Washington). The copies of old newspapers showing events in American history are especially interesting. Normal opening times are kept. There are gardens and a patio at the back where children and dogs are welcome (but not unaccompanied!).
Telephone: 01295 760389.

How to get there: Sulgrave will be found towards the south-west corner of the county. It is six miles north-east of Banbury, and nearly twelve miles south of Daventry. It is close to the B4525 road from Northampton to Banbury and can also be reached from Brackley by way of Helmdon.

Parking: Cars can be left either in the pub's own car park or by the roadside in the village. There is also a public car park at the village hall.

Length of the walk: 4 miles. OS Landranger Map 152 Northampton and Milton Keynes (GR: SP 558456).

Sulgrave is a large, old and interesting village which, on its own could provide a very pleasant circular walk adding up to 1½ miles in length. Should you wish to visit Sulgrave Manor as well then a full half day could be spent within the village.

The following walk extends beyond the parish boundaries — that is, beyond the area covered by the Sulgrave pamphlet* — but is, nevertheless, easy to follow. Between the villages of Culworth and Thorpe Mandeville a short stretch of road must be followed, but this is a quiet country lane and the occasional traffic should not spoil the enjoyment of some fine views.

The Walk

From the Star Inn proceed towards the church and turn right down Stockwell Lane. This is a gravel track leading between the houses. It bends round to the right, ending at an old pond and water mill. This dates from the 18th century and was one of the first mills in the country to grind corn using a steam engine. It is now a private residence. Before you reach this building, however, you will find a gate on your left. Through this the path leads diagonally to the far corner of the field. In the next field you keep the hedgerow to your left. In front of you is a private house with one end resembling a church tower. This is a converted old windmill. As you approach it you will see a gate to the left. On the other side a gravel track takes you to a sharp right corner followed by a sharp left corner. At this second bend you go through the gate ahead and cross the field beyond diagonally to the left. Aim for the right hand hedge of a belt of trees. There you will find a stile almost hidden by the hedgerow. This leads through to the road.

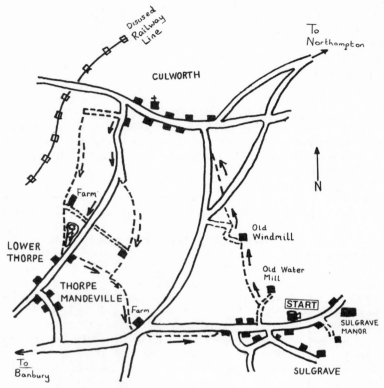

Go straight over, finding another stile half hidden by hedge and undergrowth. At first the path on the other side leads along by a hedgerow (on your left) but soon you find yourself looking across a wide, open field. Continue in the same direction, aiming for the far corner. If this field has been ploughed you may have to skirt the edge to your left. When you reach the far corner you will see a wooden fence, with a narrow field beyond, and another wooden fence on the far side of that narrow field. Climbing both these you will be on the road and close to the outskirts of Culworth village. Turn right and walk through the village. Culworth was an important settlement before the Industrial Revolution, especially amongst drovers. Two major drove roads crossed here, the Banbury Road, which roughly followed the line of the limestone escarpment from the Cotswolds to the Northampton meadows, and the Welsh Road, which came from Central Wales to the London cattle markets. There was an annual fair here and numerous inns where the cattle and sheep herders could stay, grazing their animals in all the fields around. In the late 18th century Culworth was also famous – or rather, notorious – for being the home of the 'Culworth Gang'. This was a local band of highwaymen and thieves who terrorised the neighbourhood with hold-ups, break-ins and cattle rustling. Today Culworth is a quiet, pleasant place of mixed architecture, a 12th century church and a village green.

The next part of the route involves a road walk south towards Thorpe Mandeville. Turning left after the church you pass the Culworth Post Office stores and soon leave the village behind. This is not a busy stretch of road and the views on either side are extensive. In less than a mile you reach the hamlet of Lower Thorpe, where you leave the road turning left through a gate.

The way back to Sulgrave is now clear. You cross the field up to the skyline keeping a new farm building to your left. Another gate at the top corner leads through to a field beyond. A well-marked path now runs along the edges of several fields, up and down with the fold of the hills. All the way the hedgerow remains on your left. At the far side of the third field you reach Magpie Farm. Here you meet the road – or rather, a road junction. Take the lane opposite signposted to Sulgrave.

From Culworth to Magpie Farm there are two alternative routes which avoid the stretch of road-walking mentioned above. These should be attempted, however, only by adventurous or dedicated ramblers since the footpaths are not very clear. Some fence-climbing and nettle tramping might be necessary. The shorter of these routes leaves the Thorpe Mandeville road just south of Culworth. Where the road bends right a footpath leads straight on, eventually passing the barn on the skyline. The longer route starts opposite the Culworth Post Office. To the left of the concrete lane a footpath leads to the distant farmstead of Culworth Grounds and then through a woodland to Lower Thorpe.

From Magpie Farm you could walk all the way back to the Star Inn along the roadside. But why do so if you do not have to? Soon on your right you will reach a footpath signpost. From here you can walk parallel to the road, but on the other side of the hedgerow, along the edge of two large fields. You re-emerge onto the road at the first buildings of the village. Go right to return to the inn and, perhaps, to visit Sulgrave Manor.

* Northamptonshire Countryside Services has produced a very good little pamphlet showing all the buildings of interest within Sulgrave together with the footpaths in the parish. These sketch maps are accompanied by short descriptions and historic notes.

Moreton Pinkney
The Olde House at Home

This was once called the Red Lion, and a red-painted lion figure still sits upon the shelf behind the bar. The building has largely been restored to its 17th century splendour. There are now all the features one could wish for in a country pub – old oak beams and panelling, comfortable cottage-style seats and, in the middle of the one large room, an open-sided fireplace.

Meals and bar snacks are all freshly made, and designed to suit every taste. There is a regular menu, and daily specials are chalked up on a blackboard. These include lasagnes, curries, pies, fish dishes, the latter being especially tasty, often involving cream or cheese sauces. Vegetarians would also be satisfied. Although there is just a single large bar, one section acts as a nearly-separate dining room. The Olde House at Home is a free house and serves a selection of real ales including Burton, Bass and Wychwood. Old English draught cider is also provided.

Another asset the pub boasts is that it does not keep normal pub opening times. Instead it is open all day. Morning coffees and afternoon teas are served and bar snacks are always available. Both

children and dogs are welcome, both inside and in the gardens. This is not surprising, since the pub is a friendly and accommodating place.
   Telephone: 01295 760353.

How to get there: Moreton Pinkney is 8 miles south of Daventry and about the same distance north of Brackley. It stands on the B4525 road from Northampton to Banbury. The Olde House at Home will be found on the right hand side (coming from Northampton) just around the first bend in the road as it enters the village.

Parking: There is a pub car park. Vehicles can also be left at the roadside along the village side streets. Parking along the main road is not recommended as there are many bends and traffic can be fairly busy.

Length of the walk: 3 miles. OS Landranger Map 152 Northampton and Milton Keynes (GR: SP 577493).

This walk is designed specifically to include Canons Ashby where stands a manor house of great architectural and historic interest. Part of the route there is along a medieval trackway, used once either by stagecoaches and waggons or else by drovers. The way back from Canons Ashby includes a view over the ornamental lakes in the landscaped parkland surrounding the Hall. Some road walking is involved, but much of this is along a quiet country lane with little passing traffic. Generally the way is clearly marked and easy to follow. Throughout there are good views, and constant interest created by local wildlife. Ornithologists, in particular, will enjoy the excursion. Sturdy footwear is advisable.

The Walk

Across the road from the Olde House at Home, slightly towards the Canons Ashby direction, is Plumpton Lane. This stony track runs uphill to a sharp left bend, then bears back to the right. It is an old main road once linking Moreton Pinkney with Banbury Lane, the ancient drove road which runs along the limestone hills from the Cotswolds to the Nene meadows at Northampton. The circular walk begins along this old road. You continue along it for about half a mile with views either side. The tower of Canons Ashby church peeps over the trees on the skyline over to the left.

   In due course you come to a point where the hedgerow that you have been following on your left is joined by another appearing on your right. A tall ash tree stands alone here. This must once have been quite a busy junction, for – running across the stony trackway – another ancient route can be seen. To the right this takes the form of a wide grassy way fringed by hedgerows. To the left it is merely a path

21

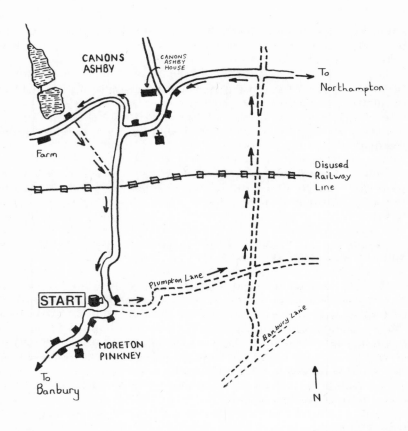

over the side of a field with a hedgerow just to the left. What seems
incongruous is that, guarding the entrance to this grassy pathway, on
either side, is a road sign. Cars are not allowed, it seems, 'except for
loading'. How any car could possibly be driven up either stretch is a
puzzle. This grassy way is a continuation of a country lane which,
further north, runs from Daventry to Preston Capes. To the south it
becomes a country lane again from Weston to Brackley. In other
words it probably once formed part of the main route from Daventry
to Brackley, as used throughout the Middle Ages and during the great
age of coach travel. This stretch could have fallen into disuse
sometime after the Industrial Revolution.

You follow this old road northwards (to the left). It crosses the
course of a disused railway line and, at the top end of the next field,
once again becomes a proper trackway, with hedgerow both sides.
There would once have been a hedgerow to your right along the

22

whole stretch but here, either side of the railway line, the farmer must have grubbed it up in the recent past.

From this point to the road, a distance of less than ½ mile, the surface of the path is variable although its route is clear enough. However, this whole stretch is a haven for wildlife so that is ample compensation.

Once on the road you turn left and soon reach Canons Ashby – a hamlet dominated by its Hall and its church. An Augustinian priory was founded here in the 12th century for 13 canons (hence the place name). Next to a priory church over 200 ft long, the monks built cloisters, a guest house, a refectory and extensive living quarters. All went well throughout the Middle Ages – too well, in fact. By the 15th century the priory had a reputation for being corrupt and immoral. It was deservedly dissolved by Henry VIII. Much of the original church was demolished, leaving just that part visible today. Opposite, on ground once occupied by the residential quarters, the present Hall was built. In 1551 the estate passed into the hands of the Dryden family who later became baronets and were to hold the estate for 400 years. One of their number – a nephew of the family head – was John Dryden, the famous poet and puritan dramatist. He was born in 1631 (at Aldwincle, in north-east Northamptonshire) and often used to visit Canons Ashby. The Hall is now owned by the National Trust and is open to the public from April to October during Wednesday to Saturday afternoons, and on bank holidays. There is, naturally, an admission charge but this is well worth the expense.

The walk continues past the Hall, through the car park and down the country lane leading to Eydon. At the bottom of the valley, opposite a farm and beyond a stone cottage, you can look across the ornamental lakes of the Canons Ashby estate, now very popular with anglers. The footpath back to Moreton Pinkney begins at the farm gate opposite the stone cottage. This crosses the field to another gate (with a grass tennis court to your right). Over the next field – a large one – you cut across diagonally, which in fact is straight on (since the field edges are not at right angles to the path). By this route you walk up to the skyline and down the slope beyond to a gate in the far corner. At that point you meet the road just before it crosses the deserted railway line. Turning right over the railway bridge you are soon back at Moreton Pinkney and the Olde House at Home further along on the right.

Hellidon
The Red Lion

A large, handsome pub this, with solid stone walls and a ground floor on different levels. Inside there are many separate rooms – two bars, a lounge, a restaurant – and lots of woodwork, with low beams and half-panelled walls. Brick inglenook fireplaces and old pictures, many with hunting scenes, add to the general old-worldliness. Interestingly – and in fact, historically more accurately – all the beams have been coloured brown instead of the more common black.

The Red Lion is a free house serving many different real ales – including Courage Directors, Ruddles and Hook Norton. Cider is on draught. Apart from bar snacks like sandwiches and rolls (all with very generous fillings, incidentally) there are various meal offerings. In fact, the menu is very wide and interesting. There are grills, steaks, meat pies, fish dishes, vegetable concoctions and all kinds of desserts. The sausages are famous!

Normal opening times are kept. Children are welcome, and not only in the gardens. This is a very popular pub, both amongst locals and people who travel some distance to sample its excellent cuisine.

Telephone: 01327 61200.

How to get there: Hellidon will be found at the western edge of Northamptonshire, close to the border with Warwickshire. It is 4 miles south-west of Daventry. It can be reached either from Staverton, on the A425, or from Badby on the A361. The Red Lion stands at the edge of Hellidon, on the corner of the Catesby road.

Parking: There is a car park at the pub. Vehicles can be left on the roadside anywhere in the village; park with care as the lanes are narrow.

Length of the walk: 4 miles. OS Landranger Maps 151 Stratford-upon-Avon and 152 Northampton and Milton Keynes (GR: SP 519581).

The first half of this walk is along a gated road from Hellidon to Upper Catesby — a narrow tarmacked lane with gates and cattle grids. This section not only provides excellent walking conditions — clear and dry even after the wettest weather — but also allows for the pushing of prams and wheelchairs without the worry of traffic. The return journey could be made by the same road. For able-bodied walkers, however, the circuit can be completed by clearly marked grassy bridleways over open pastureland. Throughout the walk only gates need to negotiated; there are no stiles to climb.

Arbury Hall, at 735 ft the highest point in Northamptonshire, is very close to the route. The peaceful Upper and Lower Catesby are hamlets rather than villages. Both have declined over recent centuries from being thriving communities. The former once had a great manor house; the latter had an important priory. Today they are almost forgotten, in this little-known corner of the county.

The Walk

The route begins through the village, so turn right outside the Red Lion and walk down to the cottages along the road to Lower Catesby. The windmill you can see up on the hill opposite the pub is now a private residence and its sails have long since disappeared. The giant telecommunications tower beyond it is a landmark throughout the walk.

Hellidon is a beautiful, interesting place with a jumble of old stone buildings clustering below the church, which stands on a central knoll. During the Second World War the church bells were silenced in common with other church bells across England. This inactivity caused a swarm of bees to make a hive inside, thus clogging up the clangers. By 1945, when the belfry was cleaned out for the bells to be rung to celebrate peace, a stock of honey had been created weighing over one hundredweight. It supplied the locals for nearly a year.

Taking the gated road leading northwards from the church, you come to the first of two farm gates which bar the way. This marks the edge of the village. Between here and the second gate, a couple of hundred yards further on, a footpath leads off to the right. You can ignore this unless of course you wish to bypass Lower Catesby and walk directly to Upper Catesby. It is an easy walk across fields and over stiles. Keeping to the road, however, you continue straight on. A cattle grid soon appears. These gates and cattle grids are necessary because the road runs through open pastures where sheep and cattle graze. The gates must be closed behind you.

Lower Catesby, which you reach in less than a mile from Hellidon, is merely a small cluster of buildings: a farm, an old stable block with a curious roof-line and central turret, and the remains of an old church. In the field nearby are the earthworks marking the site of an old priory. In fact, this was a nunnery, founded in the 12th century by St Margaret of Catesby, sister of St Edmund of Canterbury. In time, however, it became dissolute, great wealth and power corrupting the nuns, and its reputation consequently suffered. Apparently few tears were shed when Henry VIII closed the nunnery and dispersed its estates.

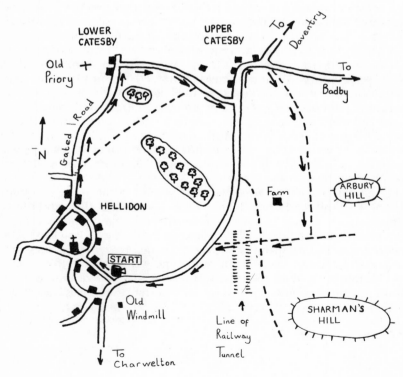

The road continues to the right and goes on to Upper Catesby (over two more cattle grids). There is pleasant countryside all about, with views across into Warwickshire. As you approach Upper Catesby you can see Catesby House on the hillside up to your half-left. It is a great Victorian pile, reputedly haunted, that dominates the landscape.

Walking through Upper Catesby you come to a sharp left bend in the road. At this point you go straight on, along a narrow gated road signposted to Badby. After a few hundred yards you come to a gate, through which, on the left, is Longridge Farm. Now, for the first time on this walk, you leave the tarmac. Striking off to the half-right you take the bridleway which is clearly marked running across the open pasture. At first you head directly for Arbury Hill, but soon you veer to the right and find yourself aiming for Sharman's Hill. This is lovely countryside: wide open grasslands and distant hill scenery. Sheep graze all about and birds twitter in the skies. The track leads through to the next field, and then to the next through a gateway. As you draw level with Highfield Farm, over to your right, you find yourself in the corner of a vast field. Go straight on, with the hedge on your left. At the bottom corner a gate to the left leads through to a hedge-fringed trackway. This leads to Badby. Do not take this, of course. Instead turn right. You now follow the second side of the field, with the hedge still to your left. In effect, you merely follow the same field around.

At the next corner a gate leads the path through some thicket. A further gate leads to another field, followed by another gate and another field. All the while you keep the hedgerow to your left. In due course the path passes through a patch of woodland, with bushes and an embankment on the right. Curving round to the right, another gate leads to a gravel track (with another bridleway coming in from the left). Go straight on. The track becomes a concrete drive, as it passes through the garden of a modern house, and then meets the road. Turn left for Hellidon and the inn.

The embankment that you saw near the end of the walk continues parallel with the road, over in the fields to your left. Here and there, along it, is a circular brick tower. This marks the alignment of a tunnel, through which once ran a railway line from Rugby to Brackley. The towers are air shaft housings. The tunnel is nearly two miles long and was constructed not because the landscape was especially hilly here, but because the owner of Catesby House, at the end of last century, would not allow a railway line to cross his estate. Such was the power of the local nobility!

Badby
The Maltsters Arms

This pub looks pleasant enough from the outside but it is even more attractive within, with low beams and oak posts, plain walls with pictures and an air of traditional charm. There is one large bar room but it does not feel like it, the settle seats being high-backed (as settles ought to be) and having the effect of subdividing the space into secluded sections. The proprietors are friendly and very happy to cater for groups of walkers.

The menus are varied and excellent value for money. The choices for main meals include the usual offerings – fish, steak, lasagne and curry – together with more specialised dishes – like salmon cooked in wine and cream. Bar snacks include different kinds of ploughman's lunches and sandwiches, both toasted and normal. All these are freshly prepared and very tasty.

The Maltsters Arms is a free house serving Ruddles Best and Marston's Pedigree ales. Strongbow cider is on draught. Children are welcome, not just in the garden but inside as well. Normal pub opening times are kept. Telephone: 01327 702905.

How to get there: Badby will be found just 3 miles south of Daventry, a little way off the A361 road to Banbury. It can also be reached from the A45 road from Northampton, turning left (south) past Weedon and via Newnham. The Maltsters Arms stands on the right as you enter the village from the Daventry direction.

Parking: The Maltsters Arms has its own car park. There is also room throughout the village where vehicles can be left at the roadside.

Length of the walk: 6½ miles. OS Landranger Map 152 Northampton and Milton Keynes (GR: SP 560593).

This is the longest walk in the book. But it is also, probably, the most attractive. There are beautiful views over hills, woodlands and meadows, some landscaped parkland of an old estate, and three pretty villages.

The Walk

Walking down Courtyard Lane, which is directly opposite the Maltsters Arms, you come to a footpath signpost at the far end. The path in question begins at the stile and runs between a fence and a hedge to a bridge and another stile. There is another signpost here. Ignoring the footpath that runs across at right angles, you go straight on: over a stile and across a field to yet another stile. There is a railed footbridge at this point, over a fast-flowing stream. This is one of the many tributaries which form the headwaters of the river Nene.

From here the route is clear. You follow along the edge of two large fields, keeping the hedgerow to your right. After more stiles and another bridge you meet the road just outside Newnham. Turn right and walk through the village, where the limestone houses gather round a central green and spread uphill to the church. Notice the most unusual open-arched tower in which, at one time, bell ringers performed in full view of the locals. Just before you reach the church turn down Manor Lane, to your right. At the bottom you will find a gate, stile and another footpath signpost. Close to this point is The Nuttery, a commercial hazelnut orchard. Ignoring the concrete track which leads into the field to your right, you strike across the grass diagonally. Initially this means going up a fairly steep grassy bank.

From here to Little Everdon, a distance of 1½ miles, the walk is not only pleasant, but interesting. You cross diagonally a number of fields, going from stile to stile. At each stile the arrow disc shows the direction you should take across the next field – although you can see the next stile in the distance if you look. This stretch crosses a valley, so it also involves two footbridges. Of interest are the parallel banks and ditches which you walk over in many of these fields. They are the

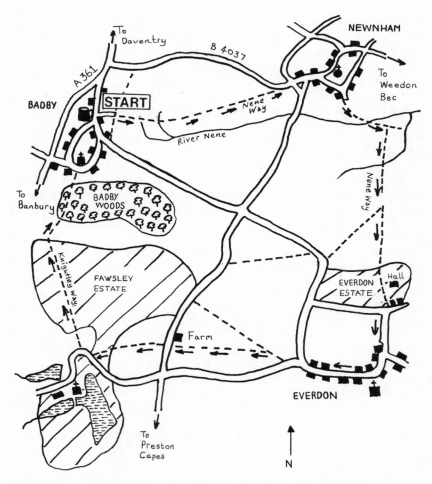

ridges and furrows left behind by medieval strip cultivation. And excellent examples they are too. Also of interest is Everdon Hall, which you pass over to your left just before reaching Little Everdon. It is a large, handsome manor house dating back to 1690.

When you reach the road you have a choice of three lanes. Take the middle one (that is, straight on), keeping the long stone wall to your right. Soon you reach the village of Great Everdon – although the 'Great' in the name is usually dropped. There you turn right and walk along the main village street.

At the far end the road bends right, and a narrower lane goes straight on uphill, signposted to Fawsley. This is the one to follow. But not for long. Very soon on the right you will see a footpath sign pointing up the grassy bank. Take this route. Beyond the stile you follow the edge of a field up to the skyline, keeping the hedge to your left. The right of way runs straight across the following two fields, using stiles on its way, but you may be required to skirt round the first of these, if the farmer has planted something he does not want trampled down. Not that it should matter if you do have to make a slight detour. The views are splendid along here, especially over to the left. As you enter the third large field, so the views open out in front as well.

You can use the tall telecommunications tower on the skyline as a directional guide. It is like a narrow lighthouse, only much higher, dwarfing everything else. By now you will find yourself walking directly towards it (to a gap in the hedge in the near distance). In the following field you head for a smaller gap in the hedge. Beyond this you follow the fence to your right, down eventually to the road, to the left of a farm. You now cross the road and walk up the field opposite, with the fence on your left. At the top you see the tower once again. Cross diagonally the next field keeping it slightly to your right. There is a good view of the Fawsley Park lake over to the left. Down at the bottom a stile leads you to the road. You are now in the heart of the Fawsley estate. Fawsley Hall has seen better days but the parkland around it is beautiful indeed. There are ornamental lakes, beech trees and an isolated medieval church. Isolated because the village it once served has been 'lost' – removed to make way for sheep grazing during the 15th century.

The home stretch is along the Knightley Way and is well signposted and well worn. The signposts are topped by large round discs and are positioned regularly along the route. The first of these will be found on the right as the road bends to the left. It is a lovely walk back – a fairly steep climb to begin with (and over a couple of step-stiles) and then a meander through an ancient beech wood at the summit. The trees are old and dying, and the wood is sparse. A beautiful, melancholy place. Beyond, the footpath begins its descent, first across a field and then down amongst the trees of Badby Woods. Soon you are crossing one last open field, and then following a narrow track as it dips between hedges and gardens. The last few yards are steeply uphill, as you climb towards the road and the jumble of old stone cottages that is Badby, with views to the west of the highest point in the county, Arbury Hill. The church is now immediately opposite. Turn right and you will soon be back at the Maltsters Arms.

Farthingstone
The Kings Arms

At first sight this looks to be a handsome late Victorian building, with ornate windows and high ceilings. But on closer inspection it is obviously much older, with low-arched internal doorways and an attractive beamed inglenook. In fact, the Kings Arms is an amalgam of ages and styles. It was first built in the 18th century but fire damage in the following century caused it to be rebuilt. The Victorians undertook the work with great sensitivity, even to the extent of using stones from the church opposite (left over when that building was refurbished). The result is a charming and original mixture of Jacobean and Victorian gothic. Deservedly the building has been listed as one of architectural interest.

The separate bars are on different levels, have their original stone floors and are heated (in winter) by a woodburning stove set in the inglenook. Tankards hang from the beams, together with copper pots, and horse brasses are used with commendable restraint. There is a broad choice of bar snacks and meals from ploughman's lunches and sandwiches to pies and scampi with chips. The Kings Arms is a free house serving real ales including Hook Norton, Wadworth 6X and

Theakston XB. There is draught cider and wine is sold by the bottle as well as by the glass.

Normal pub opening times are kept. Children are allowed into the back room and dogs are welcome (although not in the garden, which is beautifully kept). The Kings Arms is situated roughly halfway along the Knightley Way and is popular amongst walkers.

Telephone: 01327 36604.

How to get there: Farthingstone stands 10 miles south-west of Northampton and 5 miles south-east of Daventry. It is most easily reached by country lanes from Weedon, which stands at the junction of the A5 and A45 roads. The Kings Arms is towards the far end of the village (coming from Weedon) opposite the church.

Parking: There is a car park at the pub. Cars can also be left along the village street, which is quiet.

Length of the walk: 3 miles. OS Landranger Map 152 Northampton and Milton Keynes (GR: SP 613551).

The first part of the walk, from Farthingstone to Litchborough, both very attractive villages with many old stone-built cottages, follows the Knightley Way. The return journey involves short stretches of road and footpaths along field boundaries. Throughout there are excellent views.

The Walk

Turn left outside the Kings Arms and walk along the village street, admiring the varied styles of architecture on your way. At the far end, almost opposite the turning to Weedon, you will see a footpath signpost on your right. It is just past a farm and points across a field down into a little valley. The signpost is labelled 'To Litchborough' and is surmounted by a large disc. This is the symbol for the Knightley Way, the long-distance footpath which runs from Badby to Greens Norton, and you will be seeing it again, several times, on your route.

Down across the first field you reach a stile followed by a wooden bridge over a stream, leading through the hedgerow. In the next field you bear slightly left and aim for the far corner where you will find, in quick succession, a bridge, a stile and another bridge. Then bearing right you cross another field to another bridge and stile. Here there is a Knightley Way signpost. From here you bear slightly right and cross the next field diagonally to yet another stile and bridge.

All these directions may sound complicated but the route is clear. You are in fact crossing a number of fields which cover former water meadows. Between Farthingstone and Litchborough are a number of

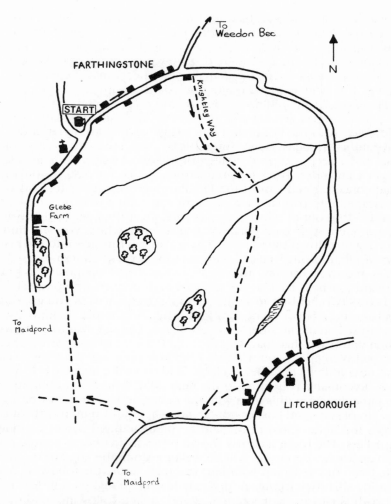

tributaries which, together, flow north-eastwards to the river Nene at Bugbrooke. The rest of the circular walk is over hills. You walk uphill to Litchborough and then round the watershed to the streams you have just crossed. This watershed – where the heads of the little valleys meet – curves in an arc-shape westwards from Litchborough.

From the last wooden bridge you cross, you walk up the next field towards the skyline and the far hedgerow. Bear left after the next stile and aim diagonally over the pastures towards the right hand side of a tall ash tree. By this time you should be enjoying the views over to your left, down the valleys whose rivers you have recently crossed. At the stile near the ash tree another Knightley Way signpost greets you. The stiles along this stretch have sliding wooden doorways built in them – no doubt for use by dogs. Owners must keep all dogs on leads across these fields, incidentally, for sheep graze hereabouts.

Over the next field you aim towards a group of tall pine trees (keeping the farm buildings some distance away to your right). There the path crosses a gravel track. Beyond the next stile you keep to the field edge, with the hedge and fence to your left. At the far end you will find a wooden bridge. Interestingly, this seems to cross, not a river, but a deep, steep-sided ditch or hollow. And yet there are clear signs of an older, brick-built construction. You are, here, on land which once formed part of the Litchborough House estate. This was landscaped into parkland two centuries ago and a little way down to your left (but out of sight) is a small lake. Over the next field you aim for a modern-style barn conversion residence, where you will find a track leading down to the road. There you can turn left into the main part of Litchborough village with its 14th century church.

The return to Farthingstone is almost as clearly signposted as your outward journey. Back at the modern barn conversion you bear left and cross two fields at an angle, climbing over fences as you go. Over the large field beyond you aim for a gate and footpath signpost you can just see on the far side. These are situated on the road to Maidford. When you reach that road you turn right. After just 200 yards, where the road swings left, you will find a signpost pointing to the right. The path now follows the side of a large field, with the hedgerow to your right. Eventually you come to the next field, where you continue in the same direction, this time with the hedge on your left. Just beyond a group of trees and bushes not far along here turn right (northwards) across the field. Should this field be ploughed and sown, continue regardless. The route is clearly shown by a way-marker – a metal disc with an arrow. Soon you will be walking along the edge of the next field (with the hedge on your left) and then across the following field (bearing slightly left). Again, this may also be ploughed but, fear not, the path is clearly signposted. You are, in fact, following the line of the watershed mentioned above.

Down in the dip two gates lead you through the hedgerow and over a ditch. The path on the far side (indistinct on the ground but clearly arrowed) leads up to the top corner where a metal gate leads through to a path between two stone houses. Beyond here a large, solid wooden door, set into a high stone wall, takes you out onto the road and the edge of Farthingstone village. Turn right to reach the Norman church (much restored last century) and, eventually, the Kings Arms.

Weedon Bec
The Crossroads Hotel

This must once have been a small, Victorian, wayside inn. Today, however, it has been expanded into a major hotel complex complete with restaurant, lounges and bedroom extensions. Beyond these, at the back, are gardens, lawns and tennis courts. At the main entrance – also round the back – plush carpets lead you to the reception area. The bars will be found beyond this. But let not this description discourage you. Inside the atmosphere is comfortable and friendly and the food is good, with plenty of choice and at reasonable prices.

The old part of the building, inside, retains something of its Victorian character. The newer areas are fitted out in 'modern old-fashioned' decor. There are high beams and low lights. Brick pillars and bare stonework give the place character, and Edwardian-style brass bar rails are seemingly everywhere. The seating is extremely comfortable, tables are large and wooden, clocks and antiques are dotted about. One glass display case contains locally hand-made pipes which are for sale.

The Crossroads Hotel is a free house. Real ales served include Bass, Ruddles, Stones and Webster's and there is house wine as well as the usual selection of French and Italian labels. Food and drink, including morning coffees and afternoon teas, are always available, for the place is open all day. Children and dogs are welcome. There is a no-smoking area and a place where children can play.

Telephone: 01327 40354.

How to get there: Weedon Bec – or just 'Weedon' – stands just 3 miles west of junction 16 on the M1 motorway. Two main roads cross here, the A45 Northampton to Daventry road and the A5 running northwards between Milton Keynes and Rugby. The Crossroads Hotel will be found at the south-east corner of the crossroads, on the left as you approach from the M1.

Parking: The Crossroads Hotel has a large car park. There is no public car park in Weedon Bec, but vehicles can be left at the roadside throughout the village (provided, of course, parking is 'sensible').

Length of the walk: 4½ miles. OS Landranger Map 152 Northampton and Milton Keynes (GR: SP 633598).

This walk combines a pleasant stroll along the Grand Union Canal with a more demanding ramble over fields and hills. In other words, the route, clearly marked throughout, offers varied conditions and landscapes together with different kinds of scenery. Strong footwear is advisable.

The Walk

Cross the A5 road from outside the Crossroads Hotel and take the lane signposted to Everdon. Just a few yards down this you will come to a bridge which is, in fact, an aqueduct (for it carries the Grand Union Canal over the road). Climb the steps to the right and you will find yourself on the towpath. Turn left and follow the canal along, with the water on your right hand side.

Walking under three bridges, as the canal bends round in a loop, you gradually leave the boating crowds behind. You pass beneath a line of pylons once and then again a little further on as the line of the canal swings the other way. Then, at the next brick-built hump bridge (Number 32 – for all canal bridges are numbered) you finally leave the towpath. Walk up to the road. Turn left if you wish to go into Nether Heyford, with its expansive tree-lined village green, and inspect the 13th century church; turn right if you wish to continue the circular walk uninterrupted.

Crossing over the canal you walk past a group of cottages and find a footpath signpost on your right. it is just before the road bends left and next to a Water Board electrical sub-station. Two stiles will bring

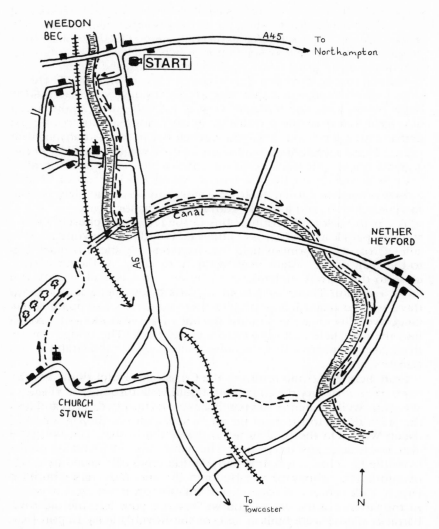

you into a field where the path leads onwards with the hedgerow on your left. After the next stile you bear left, down the edge of the field. The railway embankment is now in front of you. Follow this embankment along a little way until you find a stile, almost hidden by undergowth. This leads through to a dark, long, narrow tunnel. You may have to duck as you walk through.

On the far side turn right. A very pleasant little path now leads you through the trees, with the railway line to your right. Beyond the next stile, which leads into a field, you turn right and walk up the grassy bank. You are now standing at the top of an old, disused, railway embankment. The railway still in use, which you have been following has swung away from you – it is visible over to the right.

The walk along the derelict embankment is very pleasant. There are trees and undergrowth either side and occasional views across the fields below you. The birds are very active and noisy. At one point you have to bypass the remains of an old bridge. In due course the embankment levels out and you can see the main road ahead. Bear right, behind a small brick-built store shed, to where a gate leads onto a gravel track. This leads up to the road (which is, in fact, the A5).

Cross straight over the main road, taking the lane up to Church Stowe, otherwise known as Stowe-Nine-Churches, which has a Saxon towered church, and a lovely 16th century manor house.

The path back to Weedon begins to the left of the church. Over a stile, the path leads first across a little valley, and then, beyond another stile, across the enormous field that stretches out ahead of you. Aim to the right of the distant trees in the next valley. At the far corner, close to the railway embankment (the one, that is, still in use), you cross a stream. There used to be a plank bridge here, and perhaps there will be again, but at present there is merely a stepping stone. Once over this stream you follow the line of the embankment through into the next field and right onto a gravel track. The bridge now in front takes you across first the railway line and then the Grand Union Canal.

From here you could return to the Crossroads Hotel all the way by towpath. But to vary the route you should walk through the village of Weedon. Walk along the towpath a couple of hundred yards and take the steps down to the road below, where you see the sign marked 'Nene Way'. On the road turn left under the bridge. The village of Weedon is large and interesting. The name 'Bec' incidentally, comes from the fact that, during the early Middle Ages, the estate here was owned by the Abbey of Bec Hellouin in Normandy. The church is largely 19th century in date, except for the tower which is Norman. At the far end of the village you will see, on your left, the old royal barracks. These were built in 1803 as the Royal Military Depot. Here was the last-ditch defensive base in the event of an invasion by Napoleon. This site was chosen because it is, almost, the farthest point inland in all England.

Go under the railway line and the Grand Union Canal and retrace your steps to the Crossroads Hotel the other side of the A5.

Pattishall
The Red Lion

The Red Lion is an attractive, unpretentious building dating back to the early 17th century when it was a coaching inn. Inside the character is more genuinely old-fashioned than you often get nowadays. The oak beams really do look as though they are holding up the ceiling. There are two separate bars, one with games and the other with a 'lounge' atmosphere. The inglenook fireplace must be very cosy in winter when the logs are ablaze.

As this is a Grand Metropolitan establishment, the real ales served include Ruddles. But Hook Norton Bitter is also available as a guest beer. Strongbow cider is on draught. Standard fare is offered, both for meals and snacks. The home-made pies are a house speciality and very good they are too. The same family has been running the Red Lion for over 50 years. It is a comfortable, friendly place. Both children and dogs are welcome, and dirty walking shoes are not frowned upon. The pub maintains normal opening times and serves food every day including Sunday.

Telephone: 01327 830259.

How to get there: Pattishall is 7 miles south-west of Northampton, just off the A5 road between Towcester and Weedon Bec. The Red Lion will be found actually on the A5, in that part of the village called Fosters Booth. It is on the eastern side of the road – to the right as you travel northwards.

Parking: You can park in the pub's ample car park. Otherwise it is not advisable to park on the main road – indeed, it is forbidden. You can, however, leave your vehicle at the roadside almost anywhere in Pattishall. The village is not busy.

Length of the walk: 2½ miles. OS Landranger Map 152 Northampton and Milton Keynes (GR: SP 668540).

This short circular walk links three villages, Pattishall, Astcote and Eastcote, each with its own distinctive character. The footpaths used are clearly marked and well signposted. They run across fields and involve numerous gates and stiles – sturdy footwear is a good idea. The views are very pleasant and the walk is fascinating for those interested in village architecture.

The Walk

Turn left outside the Red Lion, going southwards along the A5. At the corner with the lane leading to Rothersthorpe (and, thereafter, Northampton) you will see Peggotty's Restaurant. Years ago this was a public house called 'Foresters Booth'. It stands on the site of an old shed or shelter used by foresters and huntsmen who worked in Whittlewood Forest, which was a hunting park covering the area to the south of here. The name of this old pub, of course, was corrupted into Fosters Booth, the name of this part of Pattishall.

Just beyond Peggotty's Restaurant, on the left hand side of the A5 is a footpath sign. From here the footpath leads diagonally across a large field. At the far side you come to a stile. At this point one path comes in from the left (having followed the hedgerow up from the Rothersthorpe road) and another leads straight on, across the field on the other side of the stile. You take neither. Instead turn right, before the stile, and follow the edge of the field with the hedgerow on your left. Into the next field, and roughly level with the farm up to your right, the hedge you have been following suddenly ends.. Ahead is a large, open field. Continue in the same direction (that is, straight) and soon you find the path bends slightly to the left, to reach a stile at the far side. Over this you then follow the hedge down to your left to another stile. In the next field you skirt the field corner, aiming to the right of a short line of poplar trees. You will soon see a gate, next to a house in the corner. Once through this gate you turn right. The path now runs along between two lines of hedgerow. At the end is another stile. Cross the next field (only a short distance) to a stile next to a house on the left. Thereafter the path runs around a fir tree hedge and onto a gravel lane. This leads down past some attractive cottages to the road.

The old style red telephone box here, and the triangular green fringed with stone cottages, presents a pleasant scene. This is probably the oldest part of Astcote, which grew largely during the Industrial Revolution. The few old cottages are vastly outnumbered by Victorian brick buildings. It once had three shoemaking factories. Students of industrial archaeology will notice the various remnants of the village's commercial past. Turn left at the road and proceed past the handsome Methodist chapel on your left. Shortly after this, over to the right, is a footpath sign. Not a stile this time but a 'kissing gate' leads through to the field. Now the path crosses diagonally, over the field to the skyline. At the top a farm gate leads into the next field.

Now bear slightly right and, bypassing the concrete farm store building, aim for the trees down in the valley at the far side. This is a pasture field. You will notice that part of it seems to be ridged, with parallel banks and ditches running downhill. These are the remnants of the old strip field system of farming as practised in the Middle Ages. Here the ridges and furrows have survived because the land has not been ploughed since that system was given up 200 years ago.

Keeping the houses of Eastcote, up on the skyline, to your half-left, you will descend this field to a point where a stile leads through to a plank bridge over the stream. Depending on time of year this stile can be half-hidden by the undergrowth, so keep your eyes peeled. Once across the stream, you walk across the next field to a gate at the top, which you will find to the right of some new houses. Through this gate, or over the stile next to it, you find yourself on the road. Turn left down into the village, which is typical of an old, stone-built agricultural settlement. There are lovely limestone cottages here with thatched roofs and many well-kept gardens, also some picturesque farmyards, so do not hurry along this next stretch. The pretty Eastcote Arms will be on your left. Beyond here the lane rises to a crossroads. Walk straight over.

The last stretch of footpath, taking you back to Pattishall, starts on the other side, a little way along on the left. Over the stile the path runs diagonally down into a little wooded valley, where you will find a plank bridge across a stream. Beyond is a stile and gateway leading the path back onto the road. In effect, this last stretch of footpath has cut a corner off. In wet weather you may prefer to walk down the road to the T-junction and then turn left.

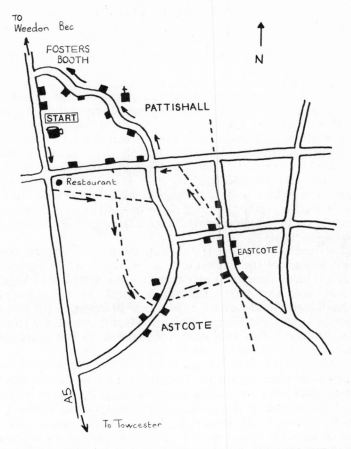

Returning to Pattishall you will come to a crossroads. If you go straight on you arrive back at Peggotty's Restaurant. If, however, you want to look round the village and its church you turn right. Pattishall is a large community with a mixture of old and new houses, some built of stone, others of brick. Little lanes lead off the High Street and the village green provides an attractive and quiet corner. The church – standing on a raised grassy knoll – has some Saxon work in the nave and a Norman chancel arch. The lane meanders around amongst the cottages. Eventually, it will lead you back to the A5, where a left turn will bring you back to the Red Lion.

Potterspury
The Old Talbot

A 'talbot' was once a breed of hunting dog, and such an animal is shown on the coat-of-arms pub sign here. Part of the existing building dates back to 1713 and the pub retains much of its old charm. In the 18th century it was an important coaching inn, standing as it does on the A5, formerly Thomas Telford's main road from London to Holyhead.

Today the Old Talbot is owned by the company Chef and Brewer Ltd and so prides itself on its food as well as its drinks. Meals and bar snacks are always available, with full menus being offered for each. There is a wide range of filled jacket potatoes and these are very popular amongst regulars. Real ales served include Ruddles Best and Webster's Yorkshire, whilst a good selection of wines and ciders would satisfy non-beer drinkers.

The lounge, public bar and dining room are all decorated in traditional style, with the former two rooms being warmed by open fires in winter. There are gardens and child facilities. Normal opening times are observed. The Old Talbot is a friendly place and caters especially for families with children. Talbot dogs are now, sadly, extinct but other canine varieties are admitted to the bar, but not to those areas where food is served.

Telephone: 01908 542124.

How to get there: Potterspury is close to the Buckinghamshire border in the south-east corner of Northamptonshire. It stands on the A5 just north of Milton Keynes and 5 miles south-east of Towcester. The Old Talbot will be found at the edge of Potterspury village, on the right hand side of the A5 as you travel northwards.

Parking: The Old Talbot has a very large car park. Vehicles may also be left at the roadside anywhere in the village, provided no obstruction is created.

Length of the walk: 4½ miles. OS Landranger Map 152 Northampton and Milton Keynes (GR: SP 753435).

This walk offers varied scenery and interest with the way being firm underfoot and generally well signposted. The route includes two interesting villages, a stretch of towpath along the Grand Union Canal, the remnants of a deserted medieval settlement, and a section of the Grafton Way. Some attractive countryside is crossed (be prepared for stiles and gates) and pleasant views are obtained. Keen walkers may wish to increase the total length of the walk to 7 miles by keeping longer to the canal towpath and taking in the pretty village of Cosgrove with its hall, priory and canalside cottages.

The Walk

From the Old Talbot, walk along the A5 northwards. It is a busy road, but there is a pavement, so this stretch is perfectly safe. This section of the A5 is especially straight, you will notice – a reminder that it follows the line of the old Roman road Watling Street, which ran from London to Wroxeter in Shropshire.

A little way along, at the corner with the road leading right to Yardley Gobion, is the Super Sausage Cafeteria. This is an excellent example of the kind of transport café that has become, sadly, a rarity in modern England.

Just before the Super Sausage, and indeed, just before the detached house close by, a footpath leads off to the right. There is no signpost here but a stile leads to a path along the side of a horse paddock. Another stile then leads to a path which runs down the edge of a field, with the hedgerow to your right. This path in fact goes almost in a straight line to Yardley Gobion. You climb over a fence, cross a large field, through a belt of trees where a stream flows, and then along the side of two more fields keeping the hedgerow to your left. Along this stretch you will see the tower of Potterspury church over to your right. Eventually you climb a stile and find yourself opposite the Yardley Gobion Recreation Centre, a newly-built sports hall. The track here takes you down to the village. The part of Yardley Gobion you see first is not its most attractive. To reach the old end follow the road round to your left, and then, at a T junction turn right. Alternatively, you could cut the corner off and go down Vicarage Road and then along a circuitous alleyway. It is an interesting village architecturally, with a pleasant mixture of stone, brick, slate, tile and thatch.

Taking the lane towards Grafton Regis you will soon come down to the main A508 road. Cross straight over this and continue down a metalled lane towards Old Wharf Farm (ignoring the signs telling you

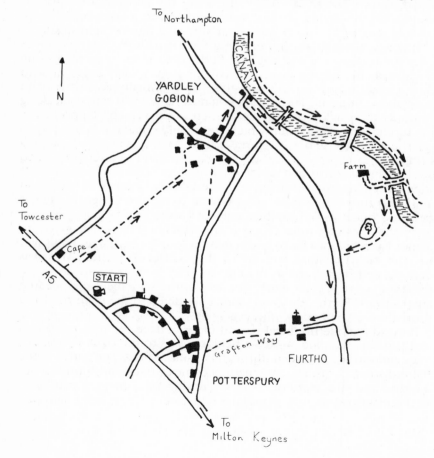

46

that this is a strictly private road). A short way down, on the right is a gate leading into a grassy field. For the next 300 yards the route is not especially clear, despite the fact that you are following the line of a bridleway. Across the next three fields (and through the same number of gates) you continue in a straight line, keeping the canal to your left. Aim for a bridge with black and white painted railings. You could, thereafter, continue in the same direction, across more fields. But it is easier if you cross the bridge and, having climbed over a wooden fence, drop down to the towpath. Follow this for ¾ mile, now with the canal on your right.

Unlike other stretches of the Grand Union Canal, this section is very quiet. Only a few narrow boats pass by. Over to the left, across the flood plain of the river Tove you can see the tall spire of Hanslope church on the skyline. In due course you reach a brick-built hump-back bridge with – over on the far side – a derelict farmstead.

Unless you wish to continue along the towpath to Cosgrove, cross over the bridge here and you will find a clear track. This runs along the west bank of the canal for a while, but eventually bears right to pass a small woodland. Beyond this you eventually reach the main road, the A508 again. Turning left you now have a 500 yard walk along this busy thoroughfare. Fortunately there is a pavement. Opposite the left turning to Cosgrove (up which you would come if you had stayed on the towpath and then turned right at that village) there is a bridleway signpost pointing to Furtho and Potterspury and announcing that it is part of the Grafton Way. This is a long-distance footpath created by Northamptonshire County Council. It opened in 1975 and runs for 12 miles from Greens Norton to Cosgrove, across farmland once owned by the Dukes of Grafton.

By the side of young chestnut trees this lane now takes you to Manor Farm, various barns and stables, a couple of cottages and (over to your right) all that remains of the village of Furtho. This was depopulated during the 17th century: only a church and dovecote remind us of its former glory. The rest of the settlement disappeared after Edward Furtho enclosed the parish, diverted the main road and turned the estate over to sheep grazing.

Beyond a modern bungalow and older cottage the path continues in a fairly straight line. Across a field it passes to the right of a belt of trees and bushes, and then (through two more fields and gates) to the right of some barns. Here the path becomes a track and soon reaches the road and village of Potterspury. Turning right then left you come to the main part of the village, the Old Talbot being at the far end.

Stoke Bruerne
The Boat Inn

The Boat Inn is attractively situated by the Grand Union Canal, its stone and thatch features decorated with hanging baskets. The four bars occupy the oldest part of the building and retain their original flagstone floors and open fires. Those facing the canal are especially cosy, with murals of waterway life and an aura of old world charm. Next door is a new restaurant and the old stable block has been turned into a tea room. The bars and restaurant are open normal times and the tea room is open all day long during the summer (shorter opening times in winter). Both children and dogs are welcome.

The inn is a free house serving a wide range of real ales – Marston's Pedigree, Sam Smith Old Brewery Bitter, Theakston XB and others. Draught Strongbow cider is also obtainable, and there is a full range of wines. The menus, both in the restaurant and in the bars, are designed 'to suit all tastes and budgets'. And indeed they do! You need never go hungry – or thirsty – at the Boat Inn.

Telephone: 01604 862428.

How to get there: Stoke Bruerne will be found 8 miles south of Northampton, just off the A508 road to Milton Keynes and close to the small town of Roade. The Boat Inn is easy to find – just follow the crowds.

Parking: Stoke Bruerne does not allow parking along the roadside: everywhere there are yellow lines. There is a car park at the inn, but few other spaces in the village, so, on a busy summer weekend you may have difficulty in finding a space. Arrive early!

Length of the walk: 3½ miles. OS Landranger Map 152 Northampton and Milton Keynes (GR: SP 743499).

For such a relatively short distance this popular walk provides a surprising variety of landscapes and features. There is canalside interest, mixed woodlands, open farmland and even a stretch next to a little stream where a ford runs across. For the historian and archaeologist there is an interesting religious building dating from the 13th century and – most fascinating of all – two fine examples of 17th century classical architecture (the Stoke Park Pavilions). The paths are clearly marked and provide easy walking surfaces. What more could one wish for?

The Walk

From the Boat Inn walk to the road bridge. With the canal to your left take the footpath signposted to Alderton. Do not take the towpath. The grassy track leads down the edge of a field to the back of a canalside cottage and then bears right to run between two lines of hedgerow. The low-lying field through the hedge to your left was once a brickworks, producing building materials for the village. It ceased operating in 1920. Beyond the next gate, which leads through a hedge that was originally the boundary of Stoke Park, the track opens out into a field. In front is a double line of poplar trees. This marks the line of the old drive to Stoke Park House. For a while you follow this, but soon veer off to the right, passing the large farm buildings on your left.

Over two stiles and another field you reach a metalled track. To the left are the outbuildings of Stoke Park Farm and, beyond these, the famous pavilions (out of sight). Crossing over the track and through a gate, the path continues at first clearly along a rutted way, and then across the grass. Beyond the next gate you follow the edge of two successive fields, all the while keeping the hedgerow on your left. Down at the stream on the far side, just to the left of a patch of woodland, you will find a bridge. The views now are ahead of you, across the flat meadows of the river Tove. Over the bridge (in fact,

49

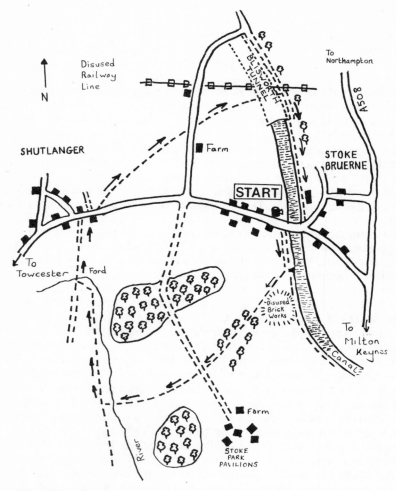

two bridges since the river divides here) and then a stile, you turn sharp right. The route is clearly marked by a footpath sign nailed to the fence.

The path now runs along the bottom edge of three large fields, with the hedgerow to your right. In the third of these fields you will find that the hedgerow has turned into a river and its accompanying undergrowth. In due course you reach a plank bridge across the river. This is an attractive spot. Ahead is a green bumpy meadow. Next to the wooden bridge an old ford runs through the river. From here, running southwards, is a wide grassy track bounded by two hedgerows. This was, probably, once an important lane, either used by coaches travelling from Blisworth to the A5 at Paulerspury, or used by drovers. The route would have run between two large estates, those of Stoke Park House and, to the west near Towcester, Easton Neston.

Walk across the meadow diagonally, passing a solitary tree on your right. A gate in the far corner leads through to a damp hedge-fringed track called, appropriately, 'Water Lane'. This brings you to the village of Shutlanger. On the right before the T junction you will see, through the trees, the large, stone-built edifice called The Monastery. Now a private residence it is an interesting and unusual building. It probably was never a monastery but it does go back to the 13th century. The front porch has a spiral stone staircase and the overall shape suggests some religious origin. Perhaps it was a monastic grange or an abbey farm.

Turn right at the T junction and continue to the footpath signpost you will see on your left. It adjoins a track leading up to the left and is shortly before you reach the last group of houses. The path crosses the field diagonally (to the right of some bushes) and passes through a gap in the far hedge into the next field. On the far side of this you will find a stile and plank bridge over a ditch. You now follow the edge of a field, with the hedgerow to your right. At the top, the path becomes a track and then meets the Blisworth road. The building over to your left here, incidentally, is the old Stoke Bruerne railway station.

Across the Blisworth road a very clear trackway winds its way across another field (which actually covers the canal tunnel far below) towards a belt of trees. Amongst these you meet a gravel lane. To your left are the remains of an old railway bridge. Turn right and follow this lane downhill, below the tall ash trees either side. In due course you reach the canal and the track becomes the towpath.

Stoke Bruerne was just a small hamlet when the canal was built during the last decade of the 18th century. Then it expanded to be one of the Midland's most important canalside settlements and a bustling and popular village. Since 1985, when the tunnel reopened, it has also become a busy centre for narrow boat traffic, and the locks here are now in constant use.

The last stretch of the walk is pleasantly taken along the canal, past moored narrow boats. As you approach Stoke Bruerne the crowds increase and your thoughts turn towards tea and ice cream. Fortunately such refreshments are provided and your walk reaches a very pleasant conclusion.

Little Brington
Ye Olde Saracens Head

This is a popular pub and well known in CAMRA circles. Deservedly so for it is a very pleasant, comfortable place with a friendly atmosphere and good food. It is a Mann's house with the selection of real ales which that suggests, including John Smith's. Draught cider is also available.

Ye Olde Saracens Head is an old, stone building of great character: low beams, brick chimney breasts with open fires, separate rooms (public bar, lounge, games room) and functional, as opposed to chintzy, furniture. To overcome the general darkness – the windows are small – little lights are strung up above the bar and around the walls, many of them coloured. These, together with the vast collection of pictures, posters, ornaments, brassware, tankards and other such bric-a-brac, create a pleasingly cluttered ambience. The meals and bar snacks are delicious. The choice ranges from the ordinary – steak and kidney pies, farmhouse grills, scampi – to the specialist – fried mushrooms and garlic dip, faggots, seafood platters. Ploughman's and harvester's lunches are offered to those not wishing for a full blowout. Desserts include various cakes, ice creams and fruit dishes. There is something for everyone.

Slightly longer than normal pub hours are kept – Ye Olde Saracens Head opens at 10.30 every morning. Children are welcome, and dogs are allowed in the garden. Incidentally, the garden is very interestingly stocked with tamed wildlife.

Linked to the pub is also the Old Barn tea room, which opens each weekday afternoon during the summer. This is a country cottage style establishment serving light meals and afternoon teas. All very civilised. Telephone: 01604 770640.

How to get there: Little Brington is 7 miles north-west of Northampton and west of the A428 road to Rugby. It can be reached by country lanes from Harlestone and East Haddon. Junction 16 is only 3 miles to the south, reached via Flore on the A45. Ye Olde Saracens Head stands at the western end of the village.

Parking: The pub has a car park. Vehicles can also be left along the roadside almost anywhere in the village, within reason.

Length of the walk: 3 miles. OS Landranger Map 152 Northampton and Milton Keynes (GR: SP 660637).

Although the walk does not cross into the Althorp estate itself, it does wind its way across farmland greatly influenced by its historic ownership by the Earls of Spencer since the 16th century. There are patches of woodland, spinneys and fox coverts especially planted for visual and sporting reasons – this area is famous for its hunting – and the old hedgerows have been preserved. Great and Little Brington are both worth a linger.

The footpaths across farmland are, for the most part, clearly signposted and marked by directional arrows, nailed to gate posts. There are some stiles, and one or two low wire fences, to climb over. The countryside is very pretty and unspoilt.

The Walk

There is a footpath which runs across the fields from the eastern end of the village (starting from the private gravel-floored road which leads to Althorp House) to Nobottle Wood where it meets the road to Harlestone. If you take this, however, you will miss a visit to Little Brington church. This stands on a hilltop outside the village and commands excellent views all around. Its air of decay has a certain melancholy beauty, and the graves and tombs are interesting and include some belonging to the Washington family. Lawrence Washington, ancestor of George, is thought to have moved to a cottage here from his manor at Sulgrave, after his family had fallen on hard times.

From the church take the road towards Northampton. This is

straight, and is aligned along an old Roman road. After a short distance turn left, down the road to Harlestone. Passing, on the left, the footpath signpost to Little Brington (pointing up the way you would have walked if you had missed the church) and then a narrow belt of trees, you come to a second footpath signpost. This is shortly before Nobottle Wood and points to Great Brington. It leads through a gate and into a large field.

The route is fairly clear, and indeed, you can see the village of Great Brington in the distance, straight ahead. The path crosses the field to the far gate and thence across the private gravel road leading to Althorp House (now to your right). Keeping the woodlands to your right you continue across the valley, through the fields. Over the last big field you follow the hedgerow, which runs parallel to the path some 50 yards to your right. This field has been subdivided by wire fences and the path runs through a series of stiles. There are good views from here, back to your right, to Althorp House and its estate grounds. The classical 18th century facade of this stately home belies its Tudor origins. Unusually the building is faced with a light grey brick and – in part – with 'mathematical tiles', that is, with tiles made to look like bricks.

In due course you reach a gate, a concrete lane and the corner of Great Brington. Continue through the village to the church, admiring the stone and thatch cottages as you go as well as the distant views. The 13th century church contains the grand Spencer Chapel where many memorials mark the graves of the Spencer family through the ages. The church tower was chosen in the 16th century to hold the southernmost beacon in Northamptonshire – one of the hundreds whose flames heralded the approach of the Spanish Armada.

Take the road opposite Great Brington church, signposted to Whilton. This is a narrow, quiet road and provides pleasant walking. You could not fail to notice the strange scenery either side along this stretch. It is a humpy, bumpy landscape of tree-topped knolls and hillocks. One of these is called Gawburrow Hill and this perhaps gives a clue to the origin of this district. These hillocks could be surmounted by ancient burial mounds – 'Gawburrow' being corrupted from 'Gawbarrow'. Some could be the sites of old hill forts or temples. A little archaeological work would solve the problem.

Along the Whilton road you ignore the first footpath signpost and take the path identified by the second. This will be seen on the left just before the farm track leading to Glebe Farm on your right. It is labelled to Little Brington. The path crosses by the side of a field, uphill to a stile. Beyond this you continue, with a patch of woodland to your left and the field sloping down to your right towards some farm buildings. You aim for the top corner, to the left hand edge of

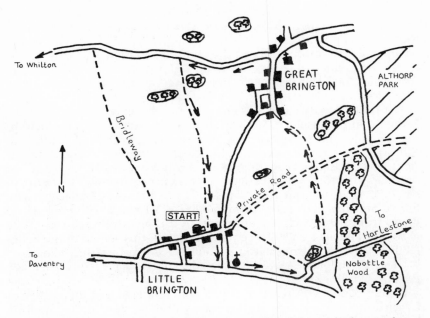

To Whilton

GREAT BRINGTON

ALTHORP PARK

Bridleway

N

Private Road

START

To Daventry

LITTLE BRINGTON

To Harlestone

Nobottle Wood

a belt of trees. Over the next stile you continue through the nettles up to a grassy trackway at the top of the ridge. Here the views ahead begin to open out. You cross the trackway and continue over the next field. The spire of Little Brington church you will see straight ahead on the skyline. The village of Little Brington is across the valley in front of it. The route is now fairly straight, across several fields. All the stiles have footpath arrow signs nailed up showing the direction of the path. Here and there the farmer may have made your journey difficult – a low wire fence here, a pile of silage there – but all the way you can see the next stile clearly in the distance. And all the way you can see the church spire on the hilltop straight ahead.

Down the valley with the hedge on your left you eventually come to the valley bottom. Surprisingly, there you will find, not a river or stream, but a ditch. Over the stile into the next field you now cross diagonally to the right. In the following field you head down towards a little tin hut. Close to this you will find a stile, a plank bridge over another ditch, and a path leading over a pasture field to the road. By the side of some garden allotments you thus reach Little Brington, with Ye Olde Saracens Head down the lane to the right.

Harlestone
The Fox and Hounds

This is a handsome, ironstone pub deservedly possessing 'listed building' status. It was fully renovated a few years back but, fortunately, its character was maintained. Inside there are black-painted beams, brick pillars and fully occupied plate racks round the walls, giving the whole a pleasant, old-fashioned feeling. The two bars and separate food lounge are not enormously large, however, and you are advised to get there early, for this is a very popular pub.

It is a free house serving a range of real ales (including John Smith's, Marston's and Tetley) and draught cider. Main meals and bar snacks are available lunchtimes and evenings (except on Sundays) and the menus are varied both in choice and price. Apart from the regular bill of fare, daily specials are offered, the choice being written up on a blackboard at the bar. The usual pies and curries are cooked, and selected vegetarian meals. The chef is especially proud of his soups and sauces. Dogs and children are not allowed in the bars but are welcome in the gardens at the back, which are attractive and quiet. Normal opening times are observed.

Telephone: 01604 843334.

How to get there: Harlestone stands just 4 miles north-west of Northampton town centre, close to the tentacles of the suburbs. It is situated on the A428 road to Rugby. Four miles to the south-west is Junction 16 of the M1 motorway.

Parking: The Fox and Hounds has a large car park. It needs it, for there are few other places where vehicles can be parked. Parking is prohibited on the main road and difficult in the village owing to the narrowness of the lanes.

Length of the walk: 3 miles. OS Landranger Map 152 Northampton and Milton Keynes (GR: SP 708644).

This is a favourite spot amongst country-lovers. And rightly so. Upper and Lower Harlestone must be two of the loveliest settlements in Northamptonshire. Old cottages, thatched and built in warm yellow stone, are dotted about amongst trees and flowers. The hills dip all around and valleys wander through the woodlands.

The walk wanders in and around the old Harlestone estate, with scenery that combines farmland with parkland. You are taken across fields of sheep, through woodlands, beside cottage gardens and across the end of an ornamental lake. You are even led across an international standard golf course. The route is very clearly marked and there are plenty of opportunities to explore other paths not mentioned in the following description.

The Walk

Outside the Fox and Hounds you walk down towards the village. On your right, up on the top corner of a house is a double sundial, one face with the inscription 'Watch and Pray' and the other face with the words 'The Hour is at Hand'. Past this you cross the stream and take the footpath to your left. It begins along the front of a cottage and runs across the field by way of a tarmac causeway. Through the next field, still walking on tarmac, you reach a trackway (opposite Autumn Cottage). Turn left and follow that track down to the stream. Immediately after crossing the stream leave the track and strike off to the right. A stile leads to a path through the woods. This re-crosses the stream and winds its way up to the edge of the lake. A pleasant scene meets the eye. From the ornamental balustrade of the bridge you look out over the sheet of water, to the left is the golf course, to the right the club house. This whole district is, in fact, the old Harlestone estate. Once owned by the Andrews family, and later sold to the Spencers of Althorp nearby, the parkland was landscaped by the famous Humphrey Repton in the early 19th century.

Across the bridge you bear left (away from the golf course) and back into the woodland. The path now winds its way back to the track you

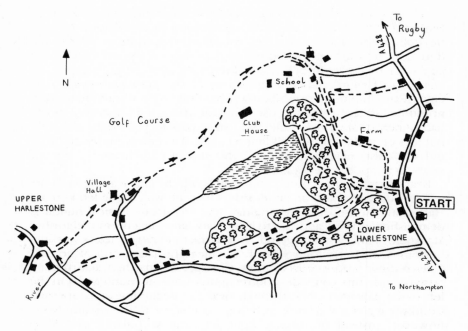

left earlier (at the stream) but further uphill. Turn right then right again, taking the route between two patches of woodland. Across a clearing (noticing the attractive cottage over to your left as you walk through) you come to a gate close to a short row of houses. Continue onwards in the same direction, crossing a gravel lane and along a track, still with woods either side. At the farther gate you enter a field, with the woods continuing on your right. It is a very clear path and brings you to another gate and the road into Upper Harlestone.

But you do not walk along the road. Almost immediately after stepping onto it, you turn right along another footpath. Ignoring the track which runs down to some houses, you take the path across the grass. This runs alongside some back gardens and then down to the bottom corner of the field. Here you will find a thatched cottage on your left. Cross the road and continue roughly in the same direction as before. Finding the way now becomes easy, for the path across the fields has been tarmacked. Nevertheless, it is a very attractive walk with the cottages at Upper Harlestone up to your left, and a little valley down to your right. Often there are sheep grazing in this field – a rural scene indeed.

The tarmacked path leads up to the village where it meets the road. Turn right and, very shortly, right again. Another tarmacked path now leads along the other side of the valley, eventually bringing you to the Harlestone village hall and playing fields. Passing in front of the hall, but behind the cottages ahead of you, the path continues in the same direction. It is still tarmacked. From here there is a good view of the lake over to the right. The next stretch crosses the golf course, so beware of flying balls. You cross one of the fairways towards the church and behind the club house. That building is ultra-modern but, no doubt, suited to its purpose. Far more attractive, however, is the half-ruined stable block which you soon pass to your right. A lovely but forlorn yellow stone building set around a central courtyard. Why did they not repair and convert this into a club house instead of erecting a modern new one?

Bearing right at the church you walk down the lane leading from the graveyard, with a wall on either side. Over the wall to the left you see Harlestone House. Not the original one – a great classical building, demolished in 1940, and said to have been Jane Austen's model for her Mansfield Park – but grand and attractive nevertheless. At the bottom, with Harlestone School to your right, is a group of houses. One of these, opposite, is Autumn Cottage. Taking the track running down beside this you will soon recognise your surroundings. On the left is the gate you came through near the beginning of your walk. Continuing along the track, as before, you come to the stream. Now, however, instead of turning right into the woodland, you keep straight on. To your left is a farm, to your right an old road-side well, half buried by undergrowth. Through the gate you continue with the trees on your right.

You now come to another place you should recognise. To your right is the stile you crossed over earlier, having seen the lake close at hand. Now, instead of turning right, to take the route between the two patches of woodland, you turn left. The path leads over a grassy field with the estate wall to your right hand side. In due course you arrive at a gate, which opens onto a gravel lane. Continue along this, between the cottages, and you come out at the main road almost opposite the Fox and Hounds.

Crick
The Red Lion

This is a stone and thatch building believed to date back to the 17th century. Despite many changes made over recent years the decor is still attractively old-fashioned, with a lot of wood and bare stone walls. In winter months two roaring fires burn in the open grates, one log and one coal.

The Red Lion prides itself on its food, and well it might. Lunchtimes and evenings have different menus, but always the choice is wide. Local fresh vegetables are prepared every day. Both bar snacks and full meals are offered – chicken, curry, lasagne, salads – the home made steak and kidney pie is especially toothsome. On Sunday lunchtimes only sandwiches and ploughman's lunches are offered – the chef being given a well-earned day off.

It is a free house serving a selection of real ales including Webster's, Ruddles and Hook Norton. Draught cider (Strongbow) and various French wines are also served. Normal pub times are kept. Dogs and children over 14 are welcome. Outside there is a paved beer garden and a lawn where young children can play.

Telephone: 01788 822342.

How to get there: Crick will be found 6 miles east of Rugby and less than 1 mile east of Junction 18 on the M1 motorway. The A428 road to Northampton passes through the edge of the village. The Red Lion stands on that road, to the right hand side (south) coming from the motorway.

Parking: The pub has a car park, approached through an arch in the building. Parking is not allowed on the A428 but there are a couple of large lay-bys. Vehicles can also be left at the roadside in the main part of the village.

Length of the walk: 5 miles. OS Landranger Map 140 Leicester and Coventry (GR: SP 590724).

This is a very easy walk, almost entirely over level ground. It is therefore suitable for those who dislike climbing hills, as well as for those who find slopes difficult.

The route is to Yelvertoft and back. The outward journey (2 miles) is by way of a clear bridleway over fields – with gates and not stiles to negotiate. The homeward journey (3 miles) is along the Grand Union Canal towpath, with ample opportunity to observe wildlife.

The Walk

From outside the Red Lion you turn right (eastwards) along the main A428 road. Some 300 yards along you come to a signpost on your left 'Bridleway only to Yelvertoft'. This is the beginning of your route. The track runs along the edge of a grassy field with the hedgerow to your right. At the far side a gate leads into the next field, this time the track crossing the middle, the line marked by wooden stakes. Through the next gate the track follows the side of a field, now with the hawthorn hedge to your left. In due course you cross a bridge over the canal.

Linger awhile here and enjoy the wide views. Behind is Crick village and the spire of its old church. To the west are the aerials of Rugby radio station (familiar to those who travel frequently along the M1 motorway). Ahead of you, slightly to the left and just a few fields away, is Crack's Hill. It is not very high but it is imposing, especially with its trees scattered around the summit. From the top there are splendid views all around, if you have time to stroll up and enjoy them. Amongst the trees you may notice that the ground is slightly ridged and the pasture is bumpy. Some people say that Crack's Hill is the site of ancient Iron Age hill fort – an old Celtic encampment. No map shows it as such but this does not exclude the possibility. Many archaeological sites in England are not marked on maps; they are too numerous for the Ordnance Survey to plot comprehensively.

Beyond the canal bridge the track continues straight ahead. At first the hedgerow is to your left and then, through the next gate, it is on your right. Crack's Hill is now immediately up to your left. After the next gate the hedgerow is back on the left. Through yet another gate the path becomes much clearer as it has been fenced in by the local farmer. Soon you arrive at the second bridge over the canal. Not such an attractive bridge this one. The last one had been a brick-built hump-backed effort, possibly of the same age as the canal below it. This one, however, is level and fenced in by metal barriers. Altogether more recent!

From here the bridleway becomes a firm gravel lane, with a tall hedgerow either side. This leads directly to Yelvertoft, passing on its way, two barns and the village cricket pitch complete with pavilion. At Yelvertoft you come out at the road almost opposite a most interesting little building. It is brick-built and surmounted by a miniature belfry. The windows are mullioned and on the face of a

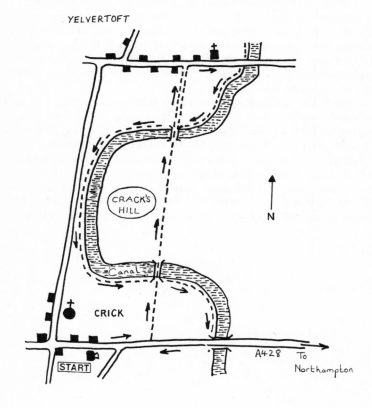

sundial over the old doorway is the date 1792. It was probably, once, the village school. Turn right along the road, passing the attractive church a little way down on your left. Do go in and have a look round. It is a large 14th century building with – unusually – three aisles. The marks on the pillars of the sedilia are said to have been made by Cromwell's troops, who sharpened their weapons on the stonework.

Further along the road, outside the village, you will come to the canal. At the bridge bear left, down the track to the water's edge, and then right, going under the bridge. This towpath will lead all the way back to Crick. This is a lovely stroll, from here onwards. Along the path once trodden by horses, as they pulled the canal barges and narrow boats, you see the countryside at close quarters. No traffic noise, but only the sound of water. From time to time a boat comes by, and you pass the time of day with the occupants. To the right is a thick hedgerow; to the left (across the canal) the fields rise up to the far horizon. There is much bird life all around. If you are very lucky you might see a kingfisher. There are two great bends in the canal and five bridges to go under before you reach Crick. Along one short stretch you are joined by a country road, on the other side of the hedgerow, but you might not be aware of the fact. It is not a busy road and few, if any, cars will pass. Crack's Hill you now pass to your left – and its potential as a defensive site is even more obvious. Surely the ancient Celts made use of it?

You reach the main road into Crick (the A428 again) just before Crick Wharf and Edwards Restaurant. Turn right and a short walk will bring you back to the Red Lion. The rest of Crick is worth exploring if you have the time. It is a large, busy village with a mixed collection of buildings, in stone and brick and of all ages. At the corner of the churchyard is a curious shelter building, thought to have been used by priests in the past. They would stand under it whilst administering burials. Archbishop Laud, who was martyred in 1644 for his beliefs, had been rector of Crick, before ascending to fame and misfortune.

Welford
Elizabethan Restaurant

Despite the name this is a pub, with a restaurant attached. In fact, there are two bars, one with games including a pool table, and one which is more like a lounge. The dining room is reached through the latter and there is a small garden at the rear.

This is an old building, and the interior is pleasantly decorated with black-painted beams, a large stone fireplace and hanging copper and brassware. But the decor is not obtrusive. The walls are plain and the ornamentation subdued. Around the bar are various memorabilia of celebrities and these provide an interesting backdrop.

The Elizabethan Restaurant is a free house serving many different real ales, including Flowers, Jennings and Morland. Cider is on draught.

The food offered ranges from bar snacks (sandwiches, rolls) to light meals (jacket potatoes, omelettes, shepherd's pie) to main dishes (pasta courses, chicken, steaks, fish). Vegetarians are also catered for with such items as mushroom stroganoff. The pub opens during normal times but longer on special days.

Telephone: 01858 575311.

How to get there: Welford stands at the edge of the county close to Leicestershire. It is 8 miles south-west of Market Harborough and 15 miles north-west of Northampton. It is situated on the A50 road, not far from Naseby and the A14 road (A1-M1 link). The Elizabethan Restaurant will be found at the southern end of the village.

Parking: There is a car park behind the pub, close to Welford Church. Vehicles can also be left at the roadside along the village side streets. Parking is not recommended along the main road.

Length of the walk: 2½ miles. OS Landranger Maps 141 Kettering and Corby and 140 Leicester and Coventry (GR: SP 641803).

This walk provides a stroll round a reservoir with an optional extension to search for the site of a medieval village. For those interested in wildfowl, there is ample to see: geese, ducks, herons, moorhens, coots. There are marshy reed areas around the lake and these too are rich in wildlife.

The Walk
The first part of the walk is downhill along Welford High Street. This gives you an excellent opportunity to explore Welford which is an interesting and attractive village, but not pretty or tranquil like other villages mentioned in this book. There is a pleasing mixture of buildings down the main road, from medieval to Georgian and Victorian, some of stone, others of brick. To the left, slightly away from the noise of the traffic, is the church – once a chapel connected to Sulby Abbey. Indeed 'connected' is the operative word, for legend says that an underground tunnel linked the two buildings. All along the High Street are a number of pubs. Apart from the Elizabethan Restaurant there is the Swan, the Shoulder of Mutton and, down at the bottom close to the canal, the Wharf House. The last named is a curious castle-style building containing mementoes of the nearby airfield, northwards towards Husbands Bosworth, used during the last war. Welford stands midway between Northampton and Leicester and so, during the 18th and 19th centuries, became an important stagecoach centre; at one time there were seven inns along the High Street.

At the bottom of the hill, just before the main road crosses the canal, there is a turning to the right. This is the road to Naseby. A little way up here, on the left, is a large public car park (a broad expanse of gravel). Behind this, up on a grassy bank, is a wooden gate. This is the beginning of the footpath. It is a well-marked track, fenced in on the right with a field beyond, and wooded on the left. You will see glimpses of the reservoir through the trees and, every so often, a

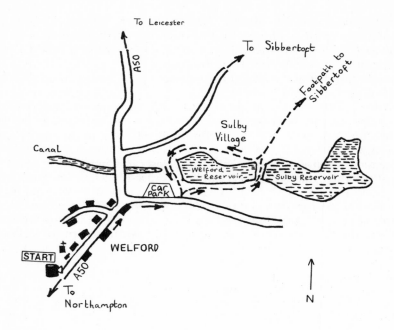

pathway leads down through the undergrowth to the water's edge. In due course the track opens out and you see the broad expanse of the reservoir in front. We are, here by the reservoir, at the top end of the Welford arm of the Grand Union Canal – and, indeed, the water feeds into that waterway, keeping the levels up. Technically speaking there are two reservoirs here, divided by a wide concrete barrier or dam. To the left is the small Welford Reservoir, to the right is the much larger Sulby Reservoir. You could, if you wish, make your way along the shores of the latter but progress would be slow since the path is not clear and the marshy undergrowth could make progress uncomfortable.

Your route leads between the reservoirs, along the top of the concrete barrier. At the far end – if you intend to search for the lost village of Sulby – you will continue in the same direction following the footpath to Sibbertoft. This takes you across a field at an angle. The best time to look for a deserted village is in the late afternoon when the sun is low in the sky. Then the long shadows pick out every nuance in the landscape – the lumps and bumps in the grassland, the ridges and hollows, which once formed the foundations of cottages and village streets. Good hunting! Today Sulby is a scatter of detached houses and farms (both old and new) connected by a network of private lanes. In the Middle Ages, however, it was a thriving community with a church and several hundred inhabitants. The monastery, to which the village was attached, stood a mile to the south, close to the Welford-Naseby road.

If you turn left at the end of the barrier, a path leads you down into a shrubby woodland – be careful of the nettles. The way is clear, however, and soon you pass some old and ruined waterworks buildings. Shortly afterwards you climb over two wooden fences – the second one by a stile – and find yourself back in the open. The lake shore is in front, and the woodlands behind you. You now have a pleasant stroll along the edge of the reservoir, where the grass is short and the banks are dry. Try not to disturb the fishermen, for they are bound to be there in abundance. This reservoir is very popular amongst anglers, permits being obtainable from the Water Authority.

At the far end of the lake you skirt, by way of a wide grassy track, back to the car park from where you turn right to return to Welford village.

Guilsborough
The Ward Arms

Named after the family that once owned much of the land hereabouts, this pub has long been an important focal point for the village. It stands opposite the 17th century grammar school building (now converted into private flats) and close to the church. Guilsborough Hall once stood nearby. Years ago the Queen Mother stabled some of her horses at the Ward Arms, not for racing but for hunting. Guilsborough stands within the district of the Pytchley Hunt.

The pub is an ancient and attractive building which does not disappoint the discerning customer. Inside all is beamed and traditional, with separate bars, a restaurant and various games facilities. The atmosphere is warm, dark and friendly. Real ales are offered (Adnams and Webster's), draught cider and a selection of wines. Full meals and bar snacks are provided, both with full menus. There is also plenty of choice for those wishing to keep to a vegetarian diet. Particular specialities – home-made meat pies, fish dishes, salads and such like – vary daily. The Ward Arms operates normal opening times. There are gardens at the back and both children and dogs are welcome.

Telephone: 01604 740265.

How to get there: Guilsborough stands 10 miles east of Rugby and 8 miles north-west of Northampton. It is 1 mile west of the A50 road. The Ward Arms will be found at the southern end of the village, on the left hand side as you approach from the village green.

Parking: There is a car park at the Ward Arms and vehicles may be left along the roadside almost anywhere in Guilsborough village (within reason!), or you might like to use the public car park at the northern end of Hollowell Reservoir, situated halfway between Guilsborough and the A50.

Length of the walk: 5 miles (3 miles around reservoir). OS Landranger Map 141 Kettering and Corby (GR: SP 678729).

The area around Guilsborough must be one of the most attractive districts in Northamptonshire. There are hills and valleys, woodlands and marshes, ancient earthworks and pretty villages, all unspoilt and unknown to tourists. There are landscaped parklands (at Cottesbrooke and Holdenby) nature reserves and, at Coton Manor, pretty gardens open to the public. There are also two reservoirs, at Ravensthorpe and Hollowell, where lakeside wildlife can be seen. The walk described here circumnavigates the latter. It is an easy route, albeit with several necessary stiles, having clear paths and no hills. Much of the landscape is open so children can run around at will to explore the woodlands and water's edge. There are many good picnic spots and − at weekends − interest is added by the many yachts which sail on the water. However, the walk would not be suitable for those who find stile-climbing difficult. All the gates encountered are padlocked − since horseriding is restricted to permit-holders − and stiles provide the only means by which fences can be crossed.

Look out for the yellow Cumberland poppy, which flowers in summer months. It is said that this wild flower was introduced into the area by William Wordsworth, who frequently paid visits to his friend the Reverend Sikes at Guilsborough Hall.

The Walk

Whether you have parked at Hollowell Reservoir or in Guilsborough, you should first stroll around the village. It is a very pretty place, and one with some historical interest. Old cottages face each other across a large village green where stands a curious barn or lock-up. At the northern end is Rose Manor, a Jacobean house of splendid proportions, and the 13th century church boasts some stained-glass windows attributed to the Victorian Pre-Raphaelites William Morris and Edward Burne-Jones. During the Civil War, Lord Fairfax and his troops were stationed at Guilsborough, before the Battle of Naseby in 1645. They camped just north of the village, close to the earthworks of an ancient Saxon fort on top of Nortoft Hill.

Walking north, away from the Ward Arms, turn right out of the

69

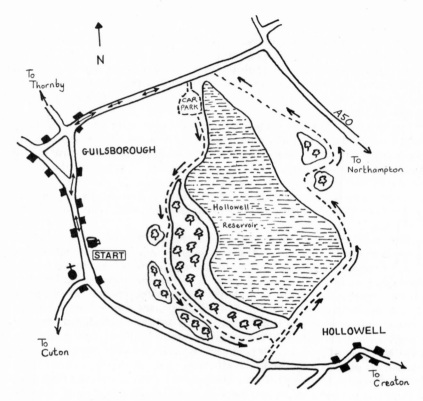

village, to the Hollowell Reservoir car park. The gate and stile at the far side of the car park lead to a footpath which runs along the left hand side of a hawthorn hedge. The pasture field to your left slopes down to the water's edge. Round the corner this footpath continues, still with the hedge on your right but now with a wood to your left. Through the trees are glimpses of the reservoir. You can, in fact, walk anywhere: through the woods, along the banks of the reservoir, over the pastures where sheep graze. As long as you keep to the left of the hedgerow which divides Water Board land from the surrounding farmland, you are free to wander. The trees are mainly Scots pines so undergrowth is minimal – allowing for very easy walking conditions. All is dark and green under the coniferous canopy, giving welcome shade in hot weather and shelter in windy weather. Towards the water's edge the land gets damper as the trees and grasses give way to marsh-loving vegetation.

The main pathway meanders along – through a gate and stile then to the right, along by the hedge and then to the left. Sometimes the lake is behind you, sometimes to the left, sometimes in front. At one point you leave the hedge and strike through the wood, along a fine nave-like stretch where the tall pines on either side tower above your head. Another gate and stile bring you to some houses, where you pass the ends of well-kept back gardens and reach a gravel track. Down to the left you will see the Hollowell Sailing Club building. Turn right up to the road.

Just before the tarmac, however, you will see a gate and stile to your left. These lead to a path which passes the edge of the sailing club premises and goes down to the reservoir dam. You are now at the southern end of the reservoir. Across the dam – enjoying the views on either side as you go – you walk over the overflow weir to a gate and stile. On the far side bear left to another gate and stile. Beyond these you find yourself in open grassland, with only sheep for company.

The way back is clear enough. Keeping the lake to your left (together with views across the valley and the occasional sighting of Guilsborough church spire peeping above the trees) you make for the far end. You will see the car park in the distance for most of your journey back. Once again, you do not have to keep to the official path. If you do, however, you will find yourself passing a clump of pine trees to your right, and then turning into another woodland towards the boundary hedge. At the far end of the woodland you come to a large expanse of pasture. The car park is now clearly to be seen ahead. Cross this pasture diagonally towards the gate at the far corner. This leads on to the road. Just before the gate, however, another path runs down to a bridge and thence back to the car park by way of the gate and stile you encountered at the very start of the tour.

Brixworth
The Coach and Horses

This is an attractive building both inside and out. The name correctly suggests the pub's origins as a coaching inn although little remains of the former stable-block behind. Much of the original character survives and the place is extremely welcoming and comfortable. There are two lounge bars and a separate restaurant, all with the traditional decor: oak beams, settle seats, 'olde worlde' ornaments, wheel shaped ceiling lights. There are gardens at the back.

It is a free house serving Ruddles and Tetley real ales. Both full meals and bar snacks are offered, each with a full menu. Meat pies, sausages, scampi and continental dishes are always available. Salads are varied and ploughman's lunches are large enough to satisfy the most hungry of walkers.

The Coach and Horses operates normal pub opening times. Dogs and children are welcome, especially if they are well behaved.
Telephone: 01604 880329.

How to get there: Brixworth stands 6 miles north of Northampton and 10 miles south of Market Harborough on the main A508 road. There is a bypass and so the main street through the village, once noisy and busy, is now quiet and pleasant. The Coach and Horses stands on this road, on the right hand side as you approach from the south.

Parking: The Coach and Horses has a large car park, but still not large enough to cope with the busy periods. Vehicles can also be left at the roadside in the village, although parking along the old main road should be avoided because of the bends. There is a gravel car park by the church.

Length of the walk: 3 miles. OS Landranger Map 141 Kettering and Corby (GR: SP 750709).

This walk incorporates a section of the Brampton Valley Way, a public right of way created by the local authority, stretching from the Brampton villages to Hanging Houghton. It follows the line of a dismantled railway (the one that ran from Northampton to Market Harborough) and its surface is wide, firm and flat, made of rolled gravel. It is therefore suitable for prams and wheelchairs. Those wishing to take the very young, or disabled, for a stroll in the country, will be able to park their cars at the car park on the Brixworth to Spratton road, mentioned in the walk description. From there, a walk can be taken in either direction along the old railway.

The Brampton Valley Way forms the central section of the walk. The rest of the circuit, from and to the attractive village of Brixworth, in Saxon times one of the capitals of Mercia, is over slightly rougher ground but it is well marked throughout and the route is always obvious.

The Walk

From the main road through the village, and opposite the Coach and Horses, take the High Street. Shortly you bear left (on the road to Spratton) and pass, on your left, the medieval stocks and the base of a 14th century stone market cross. The church can be seen up a lane to your right. On no account should this be missed. It has been described as 'the most imposing architectural memorial of the 7th century north of the Alps'. It is largely of Saxon construction. However, recent excavations have indicated that some of its structure is much older – perhaps Roman.

Where the road splits, to the left going to Spratton, to the right going to Creaton, you go straight on up a narrow lane past a house called The Firs. There is a footpath sign here. Up this lane you come to some modern bungalows. The footpath begins to the right of these, approached by the side of a garage. Once over the stile you turn left, behind the bungalows and out into the fields. From here you continue in a straight line, keeping the church spire directly behind you. Through more fields and over more stiles the path leads downhill into

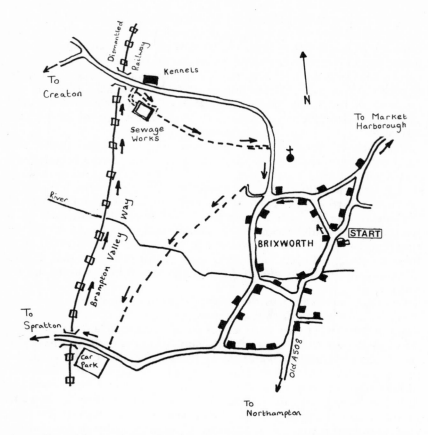

the valley. Aim to the right of the trees in the valley bottom. Beyond
a further gate you will find yourself in a broad field. The path clearly
runs diagonally, to a gate in the far side and the road.

Turning right on the road you come immediately to a large, gravel-
floored car park. This is where the Brampton Valley Way crosses the
Spratton road. There is also a picnic site here, and various public signs
advertising its own existence: access for the disabled, for cycles,
horses and so on.

Take the old railway route signposted to Creaton Road and
Houghton Crossing. Easy walking this – and very pleasant too. The
fields and meadows stretch either side with hills beyond. Up to the
right is the spire of Brixworth church. It is a puzzle why more disused
railway lines are not made into footpaths. There ought to be many like
this all over the country.

At the Creaton road, less than a mile from the car park, the track passes under the old railway bridge. A short distance further on, and before you reach a large wooden barn, a pathway leads up the bank to the road. You are very close, here, to the kennels of the Pytchley Hunt. They will be seen on the left as you walk up the road back towards Brixworth. The buildings are not especially old but are elegant in mock-Georgian red brick and set around a central courtyard. The Pytchley is one of the five famous Hunts of the East Midlands – the Quorn (in Leicestershire) is another.

The footpath back to Brixworth, however, leaves the road to the right before you reach the kennels. A sign points down a private road next to an old industrial yard. It is a concrete road but you soon leave it. Just 100 yards down there is a stile in the hedge on the left. There are now a number of fields to cross. First you aim diagonally towards the sewage works, where you reach another stile followed by a wooden plank bridge over a ditch. Then you follow the outside of the ring fence up to the corner, where another stile awaits. After crossing this one you head uphill at a slight angle towards the skyline. As you climb be sure to look behind, for the view from here should not be missed.

Over the next stile you turn right, to the corner of the field, and then left up the side of the hedgerow. In effect, you skirt round two sides of the field, to save any crops from damage. The church spire, incidentally, is now in front of you again. Soon the path runs between two hedgerows and is overhung by trees. It is clear enough but the nettles can be a nuisance. This brings you to a gate and the road. Almost opposite is a track up to the church. If you have not already done so, now is the time to take a closer look at this ancient and unique building. Return to the Coach and Horses either on the lane that leads to the Spratton road from the church or by staying on the Creaton-Brixworth road to the crossroads, where you turn left.

Lamport
The Lamport Swan

This is a large, handsome, 18th century building which began life as a coaching inn on the London to York road. It stands upon a knoll and has extensive views to the north and west. Inside, the Tudor look with beams and wooden posts is not in keeping with the age of the building, but is very pleasant none the less. There are two separate bars, open fires (albeit gas operated), and comfortable seating.

The Lamport Swan is a free house and serves a wide selection of drinks: real ale (Marston's Pedigree and Flowers IPA), draught cider and various wines, including those from Chile and New Zealand. But it is for its food that this pub is justly famous. In both its restaurant, and its bar meals, the choice is wondrous to behold. Every taste will be satisfied: there are wholesome pies, foreign delicacies, interesting salads and vegetarian dishes – all home-made and fresh. And prices are reasonable too. No wonder people come from far and wide to sample the fare.

Open at normal times, the pub has a garden, where dogs and children are welcome, and access for the disabled.

Telephone: 01601 28555.

How to get there: The pub is 3 miles north of Brixworth, on the left of the A508 and opposite the B576 which leads to Lamport village and, beyond, to Rothwell. Market Harborough is 8 miles further north, Kettering is 8 miles further east.

Parking: As well as the pub's own car park vehicles may be left in the layby on the eastern side of the A508, close to the entrance gates to Lamport Hall (parking in Lamport village is limited).

Length of the walk: 4 miles. OS Landranger Map 141 Kettering and Corby (GR: SP 756745).

This walk links two very attractive villages, Scaldwell and Hanging Houghton, and crosses some lovely unspoilt countryside. The footpaths used are not, perhaps, as clear as they might be but they are easy to follow.

The Walk

Before starting the walk some people may wish to see Lamport Hall and its estate, which stands almost opposite the Lamport Swan. It is a fine classical mansion (dating back to 1654 but enlarged and altered in Georgian times) once the home of the Isham family. Today it is run and maintained by the Lamport Hall Trust and frequently plays host to exhibitions, fairs, craft and antique markets and musical events. The gardens alone would be worth a detour.

Turn right from the inn southwards down the A508. It is very pleasant along here despite the traffic. There is a path by the road, beyond a grassy verge, and plenty to look at: to the right are glorious views westwards towards Guilsborough, to the left are glimpses of Lamport Hall, over the estate wall and through the trees. Shortly you pass the estate entrance (gates with stone posts surmounted by two white swans) and then a little further – still on your left – you reach a farm gate. Here you will find a signpost marking the footpath to Scaldwell. This is, effectively, the start of your walk.

The path first leads you through a belt of trees and thence along the outer edge of the Lamport estate (to the left and marked by a hedgerow). Soon you reach the ruins of an old barn and here the pathway suddenly seems to disappear. Fear not. The way is clear. The views have opened out and, from this spot, there is a fine prospect ahead of you. Hills and valleys, fields and woods. If you turn half right you will see, in the middle distance, the village of Scaldwell. All you have to do is aim straight for it.

Crossing the field at an angle you will find that you are, in fact, heading towards a gap in the hedge on the far side. Upon reaching that gap – in fact a gateway – you will see a clear track running forward, to the right of a hedgerow. Walking along this you will see that Scaldwell is now to the half right again. The trackway is double-rutted and grassy – evidently used by local farm vehicles. You do not, however, stay on it for long. Just before it bears right, to go round the edge of the field, your footpath strikes off more sharply to the right. From here you can still see Scaldwell and – now for the second time – you find yourself heading straight for it. Over the next three fields you cross diagonally, ignoring the field boundaries and all the time keeping Scaldwell directly ahead. At intervals you will find posts marking the way, each with a footpath arrow disc nailed up. At the far side of the third field a gate leads onto a path running into the village. Scaldwell at last!

This must be one of the prettiest villages in Northamptonshire. Nearly all stone built and honey-coloured, it has a miniature village green, a 12th century church, some ancient cottages and a plethora of beautifully kept gardens. George Clarke, the antiquarian, artist, musician and mathematician, died here in 1867 and – much more recently – the author H.E. Bates (inventor of the Larkin family) often stayed here. Scaldwell even has its own ghost – a 'Grey Lady' – who is sometimes seen wandering the lanes, dressed in a long gown and heavy veil.

Walking through the village you ignore the signposts pointing to 'West End Only' and 'East End Only' (which lead to cul-de-sacs) and keep to the road to Brixworth. Then, after bearing right and passing Sundial House (note the magnificent sundial high on the front of the building) you find the Grange, a lovely Georgian residence standing back from the road, immediately followed by Peters Lane, still to the right. Turn down here and you will find, very shortly, the footpath sign pointing left. There are, now, several stiles to be negotiated. By way of these the path leads along the side of a large and attractive garden, thence across a field (half right) to the bottom corner. After another stile you bear slightly left, keeping the hedgerow to your right, and then (after yet another stile) continue in the same direction, this time keeping the hedgerow to your left. The views, now, are to your right – the broad arable fields, stretching down, and then up, towards the woods on the skyline.

Eventually, at the far side of the second field, you come to the end of your hedgerow and are facing the wide expanse of an enormous field. Continue across this, keeping in the same direction as before and roughly parallel to a line of trees you will see way over to your left. Within about 400 yards you will reach the Brixworth to Lamport road. Turning right down this road you will soon find the footpath signpost pointing left. This leads directly to Hanging Houghton, which you can now see clearly, set upon a spur of land. You have to make your way diagonally across a single field.

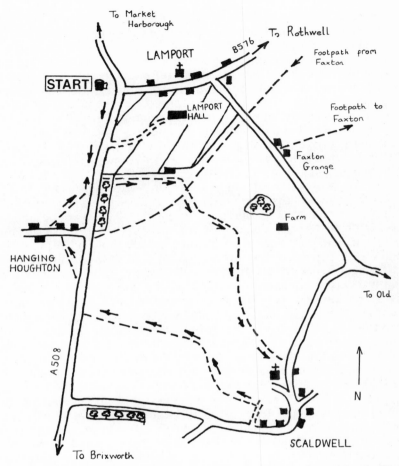

A small pleasant village this: it is quiet and leafy, and seemingly bypassed by the rush of the modern world in spite of many new houses. From the end of a shingly drive a very easy footpath leads back to the main road. Passing through a kissing gate you will see the Lamport Swan in the distance. The path runs across a high pasture field, through another kissing gate, and on to the A508 – all the way our pub starting point being seen to the half left. The walk along the A508 is but short – the less so if your meal awaits!

Harrington
The Tollemache Arms

A very attractive thatched country inn this, dating back to the 16th century. The cottage-style garden in front is full of flowers, the car park at the back looks out over pleasant countryside. The whole is beautiful to behold. The name comes from the 19th century rector of the local church, Hugh Tollemache, who is said to have bought the pub in order to close it every Sunday – thus encouraging the locals to attend his services.

Inside the decor is Tudor-inspired and glinting with horse brasses. There are separate bars, with open fires and a restaurant which occupies a room once used for laying out corpses (prior to burial at the churchyard, down the road). Wooden tables and chairs, and cushioned settles, provide comfort – although space can be limited at busy times.

It is a Charles Wells house offering real ales in the form of Eagle and Bombardier Bitters, the latter being especially bitter. There is a full menu in the restaurant and a wide choice of bar snacks. All the food is home-made and fresh. The Tollemache Arms is open at normal times and has gardens front and rear. Telephone: 01536 710469.

How to get there: Harrington is situated 7 miles west of Kettering, just north of the A14 (the M1-A1 link road). The pub faces the lane which leads to Rothwell.

Parking: In addition to the pub car park, there is ample space for vehicles to be left by the roadside along the village street. This is not busy, and the trees along here provide ample shade in hot weather.

Length of the walk: 4 miles. OS Landranger Map 141 Kettering and Corby (GR: SP 776803).

Throughout the walk, many faint signs will be seen in the landscape of varied 19th century activity – ridges and bumps in the fields, hollows and pits. With the trained eye of an industrial archaeologist there is much to discover. The irregularities in the field at the beginning of the walk, however, are much earlier in origin than the Industrial Revolution. For here there are the foundations of an Elizabethan manor house, together with its terraced gardens and ornamental lakes.

The route is easy to follow, being almost entirely along clearly marked bridleways. The countryside is open and unspoilt. Arthingworth, which is included in the route, is a pleasant and interesting village and would repay a closer look.

The Walk

From outside the Tollemache Arms you turn right along the one and only village street. There are some attractive rows of cottages along here and the pavement runs along by the side of a stone wall. Over this wall, looking out over the sweep of countryside to the west, you can see the village of Arthingworth and the tower of its church. A line of tall chestnut trees grows along here and the aspect is very pretty. Looking at this placid scene today it is hard to believe that, during the 19th century, the village was a hive of activity. On and off during that whole period test borings were made in the search for coal. The Leicestershire coalfields were not that far away and, it was hoped, the coal seams would extend to this part of Northamptonshire. They did not and so nothing was found – except, that is, the site of an extinct volcano. At the same time, limestone was being excavated hereabouts, partly for building stone, partly for lime (to be used as a fertilizer) and partly for the iron ore deposits common in this geological outcrop.

At the end of the wall is a bridleway signpost and the track leads off on the right. Through a gate and sheep pen you find yourself descending, with a hedgerow to your left and a bumpy pasture field to your right. It is in this field that you will be able to pick out the terraces and hollows which were once the Tudor estate of the Lords Stanhope and Earls of Dysart. Originally it was a monastic manor owned by the Knights Hospitallers of St John of Jerusalem, but it was

81

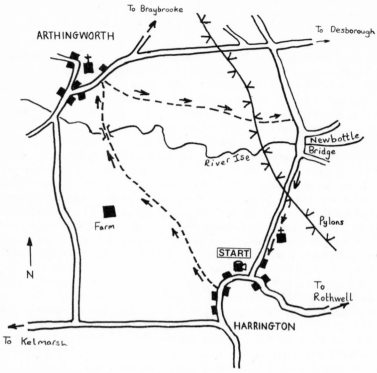

To Braybrooke

ARTHINGWORTH

To Desborough

Newbottle Bridge

River Ise

Pylons

Farm

N

START

To Rothwell

HARRINGTON

To Kelmarsh

taken out of their hands at the Dissolution. Sadly the manor house was demolished two centuries ago and its gardens turned over to sheep grazing.

Beyond this field – called the Falls Field incidentally – the track becomes a trifle overgown as it passes between two hedgerows and through some nettles. Not for long, however. After the next gate you are, once again, in an open field and walking becomes easier. The track runs up a slope, at the top of which a splendid view opens out – Arthingworth ahead of you and, slightly nearer and to the left, Warren Hill Farm up on a spur. The hedgerow is now on your right and, in the distance, you can see the track passing through another gate. And so you continue, by hedgerow-side and gateway all the way to Arthingworth, keeping the farm to your left. Soon you drop down towards the river Ise. There you will find a picturesque little bridge, narrow and brick-built, beside the remnants of an old ford. The track ends at the gate in the top corner of a field. There you join the road, where you turn left into the village. The return route begins at this

82

same gateway, running half back on yourself to the right. But look around the village first.

Arthingworth is not pretty – it is largely brick-built and has a fair number of new estates and modern bungalows – but it occupies a pleasant position. It stands on a small hill and affords views across the countryside, especially from the 12th century church. There are three attractive farm buildings in the village and some elegant lodge houses at the gates to the estate.

For the return walk, the bridleway crosses the field diagonally. Keeping the line of the river Ise to your right – marked by a line of trees and bushes – you aim for the double farm gates at the far side. Through these you cross the field beyond heading up to the grassy skyline. Over the hill the way becomes clear. The track is more definite – a double rutted way meandering across the landscape. Round the next hillspur you soon find yourself walking under a line of pylons. Shortly after this you come to another double gate and the road. These double farm gates have certainly become more common over the last few years. Their greater widths allow for the passage of the huge farm machinery now used. Massive combine harvesters can be as much as 12 ft wide.

Turn right down the road and you come to a pleasant spot called Newbottle Bridge. Here four country lanes converge, the river Ise flows under a bridge and tall trees cast their shadows down. Willows grow along the stream and all is rustically quiet. If you have time walk up the lane a little way towards Thorpe Underwood and look out over the fields to the left. You will see the remains of the old embankment, which once carried the mineral line to Desborough. Lime and iron ore were excavated around here and the deposits were taken by rail to the main line from Kettering to Market Harborough. From Newbottle Bridge you can walk up the road back to Harrington. There are tall hedgerows either side but, as the road climbs, so the views improve. On your left, before you reach the village, is the 13th century church, surrounded by a wooded graveyard. It is a fine building and boasts possession of one of the few 'vamping' horns to survive in England. It is kept in a glass case at the west end of the church. It is a brass instrument some 5 ft long dating from the 17th century. It was once used to accompany the choir during services.

A pleasant, hedge-fringed path, high up above the road, leads from the church back to the Tollemache Arms.

Great Cransley
The Three Cranes

Cranes are quite a feature of this village. The name derives from the Saxon for 'clearing of the crane', cranes figured in the coat of arms belonging to the family which once lived in the manor house here, and herons can still be seen flying around – for Cransley Reservoir is not far away. There is even a stained-glass window in the church showing cranes. So it is not surprising that this pub is called The Three Cranes.

This is the epitome of a small country pub. Inside there is just a single bar – although one end is set aside for dining – and all is traditional and dark. A log fire burns in the open grate during the winter months. In the summer customers need to spread into the gardens, where playthings are laid out for children.

It is a free house serving Marston's beers and a regular guest beer. The menu is varied with 'something for everyone' and the fare is very good and reasonably priced.

Normal opening times are kept with food every day but Sunday. Children are welcome – as is evident from the play garden at the side of the pub – but dogs are not. With such a small interior this is understandable.

Telephone: 01536 790287.

How to get there: Great Cransley stands just 3 miles west of Kettering, close to the A43 road to Northampton. To reach it from that road, however, you must first go into the village of Broughton and then take a country lane which passes under the Broughton bypass. The Three Cranes will be found on the left hand side as you come from Broughton.

Parking: Unusually the pub does not have its own car park. Vehicles can, however, be left at the roadside along the village streets. The lane leading to the church would be a quieter choice for parking space.

Length of the walk: 3 miles. OS Landranger Map 141 Kettering and Corby (GR: SP 831768).

This is an easy, fairly level walk using clear bridleways the whole way. The countryside is unspoilt, the skies are broad, and the sounds are entirely nature-based. You would never imagine that you are so close to Kettering.

The Walk

From outside the Three Cranes you take the lane leading westwards, signposted to the church. There is also a bridleway signpost, pointing to Old. It is an extremely pleasant lane to stroll along – deeply shaded and quiet. Copper beeches and yew trees keep out the light and a long limestone wall keeps you company. There are some old cottages along here. Soon you pass on the left, a wooden fence and line of trees which shield Cransley Hall, and then you can see the church, its pretty tower and spire peeping out from behind some houses. For those with spare time a visit to the church would be worthwhile. It has strong links with America. Just before the outbreak of the Second World War a service was broadcast from here to the United States. During the war, the vicar here held regular Thanksgiving Services for US troops and airmen stationed at local airfields. After the war, American soldiers presented the church with a stained-glass window. This can still be seen. It shows Roosevelt and Churchill in conference over the Atlantic Charter.

At the far end – for the lane is a cul-de-sac – is the splendid Old Lodge Farm and a small turning circle for cars. Ahead are two trackways, forming a fork in front of you. You take the right hand one. This is as clear as it could be. It is surfaced with stone and shingle and is as wide as a country lane. Motor vehicles are prohibited but walkers are not. Except for a double curve the trackway is straight, running towards the farm buildings in the distance. To the right is a dense woodland (where a footpath leads in and begs to be explored) and to the left is the hedgeless fieldscape. What a pity some of the hedgerows

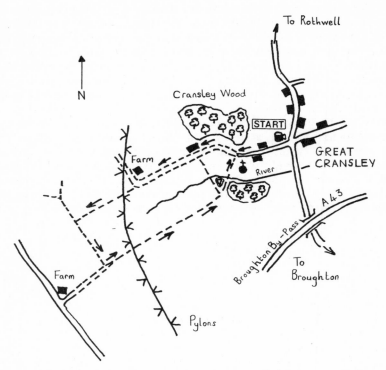

have gone along this stretch. With such a flat countryside they would have kept the winds down, let alone provided habitat for wildlife.

After passing a modern, detached residence on the right, you soon reach Squires Farm – a collection of old stone barns and an enclosed farmyard. Here the track turns right but an equally clear pathway continues straight on. This is your route – straight on and under a line of pylons. In due course the track reaches a T junction, with a large field directly ahead. Turn left and continue down to a gateway. A farm and two tall silos will be seen over to your right. At the gateway is another T junction. The track to the right would lead to the Harrington road. You turn left. This takes you back under the pylons. There is always a high-pitched buzz emanating from electricity cables – most disconcerting when you walk under them.

By now the scenery has improved. You have left the large, flat, open fields behind and you are walking through much prettier, more intimate countryside. A very pleasant little valley will be seen down to your left, with a stream and line of undergrowth marking its course. Soon you are following a short line of trees, and the land is beginning to slope ahead of you. Great Cransley church spire just peeps over the trees in the distance in front. At the next gate and stile the trackway turns left towards the modern house you passed earlier. Ignoring this you go straight on (over the stile) and down the path leading to the woodland. Your path does not, in fact, go through the woods. It runs between two separate patches of woodland. There are two more gates here to negotiate. Beyond the second gate the path swerves uphill across the field.

Here is a picnic spot par excellence! Below you are the woods and stream, ahead of you is a view of the church nestling in a valley. You can even see, from here, the long roofline of the oh-so-private Cransley Hall. A lovely spot indeed to spend a quiet hour or two.

At the top of the field, having passed on the left a small enclosed cemetery set on the hillside, the path reaches the gate. Through this is the car-turning space and the lane back to the Three Cranes.

Little Harrowden
The Lamb Inn

There has been a pub here since 1780 but the building dates back to the previous century, although in recent years there has been much refurbishment. One door from the pavement leads to a small public bar and games room. Another door leads to a lounge bar, which is on split levels. There is a separate dining area reached by steps from the lounge. The decoration is splendidly understated. There are old oak beams with plain walls adorned with just a few pictures and posters. The Lamb is cosy and friendly – and traditional in the best sense.

It is a Charles Wells house serving Adnams, Broadside, Eagle and Bombardier ales. Strongbow cider is on draught and there is an extensive wine cellar. The food offered is excellent, and very reasonably priced. There are main meals and bar snacks galore: the former including such dishes as steak, kidney and ale pie, mushroom stroganoff and vegetarian pancakes, the latter including ploughman's lunches and sandwiches with very generous fillings. Daily specials are written up on the blackboard in the lounge bar. 'Basket' meals (like sausages and scampi) are always offered, as are splendid roast lunches on Sundays. The Lamb is open during normal pub times. There is a pleasant beer garden at the back and children are not excluded.

Telephone: 01933 673300.

How to get there: Little Harrowden is just 3 miles north of Wellingborough and 5 miles south of Kettering. It stands to the west of the main A509 road which connects these two towns. The Lamb Inn will be found on the right hand side on the road to Orlingbury, coming from the main road. It is not along the High Street, which is the B574 road.

Parking: The Lamb Inn has its own car park. Vehicles can also be left along the village streets, with due consideration for other road users.

Length of the walk: 4½ miles. OS Landranger Maps 141 Kettering and Corby and (just!) 152 Northampton and Milton Keynes (GR: SP 867714).

Considering how close this area is to Wellingborough, Kettering and Northampton, it is surprisingly rural. The walk wanders through the countryside, linking the two villages of Little Harrowden and Great Harrowden with the hamlet of Hardwick. It crosses a landscape of large fields and fox coverts, of fast-flowing streams and low hills. There are wide views and broad skies. It is an easy walk to follow being mainly along gravel tracks and bridleways. The few stretches which involve paths across fields are well indicated by signposts and footpath arrow discs nailed to gates. There are no steep slopes and − unusually − no stiles.

Only very short detours are required from the prescribed route to see both Great Harrowden Hall and Hardwick. Each detour would be, in effect, a trip into 'old England'.

The Walk

From the Lamb Inn you walk up to the little roundabout and turn right along the Hardwick road. It is not an especially busy road, and there is a wide grass verge to walk on. Moreover, once off the road, the remainder of the circuit more than makes up for having to share the first ½ mile of this country stroll with motor traffic.

Just before the main road passes under a line of pylons (or, more accurately, a double line of pylons) you turn down Stonebrigg Lane. This is a gravel track and is signposted as a bridleway. The traffic noise is left behind and an attractive, wooded valley lies ahead. The track leads downhill to the stream, which it crosses by an almost invisible bridge. It then turns left, and so do you. For some little while, you continue along this track by the valley bottom, with the fields rising up to your right and the bubbling, roaring stream to your left, half hidden by the thicket. It is very pleasant along this stretch, with plenty of bird song and many a wildlife rustle in the undergrowth. Eventually the track leads into an arable field and abruptly stops. Fear not. Just a few yards short of this terminus, on the left and easily missed, is a narrow pathway leading between bushes. There is a double plank bridge over the stream and a pathway on the far side leading up a muddy bank into the field beyond. Taking these you soon find yourself on the other side of the thicket.

The next stretch involves walking diagonally across two fields. There are footpath arrow discs pointing the way so the route ought to be clear. Across the first field you head up to the skyline and towards the top telegraph pole. There are two other telegraph poles in the field but you pass these to your left. Across the second field you aim to the right of the house which you can just see amongst the trees. You emerge onto a country lane very close to Hardwick. To visit that hamlet you need to turn right and the detour would certainly be worth while. Hardwick is a pretty little place, consisting just of a church, a manor house and a couple of cottages. In the early Middle Ages it was owned by the Knights Templar; in the late Middle Ages by the Knights Hospitallers of St John of Jerusalem.

To continue with the circular walk, retrace your steps and walk down the lane to a crossroads. Go straight over and continue past a house on your left until you reach, on the same side, a signpost

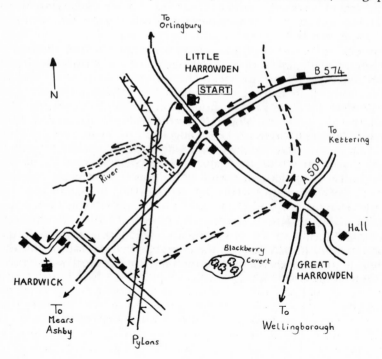

pointing the way along a bridleway to Great Harrowden. This is before the lane goes under the double line of pylons. Take this bridleway, which runs along the side of a field, with the hedgerow to your left. Soon this hedgerow ends and you are facing open countryside. The route is clear however. Continue in the same direction, going under the pylons. You will be walking between two fields – no doubt along a course once occupied by a hedgerow. Indeed, the trees growing in that long lost hedgerow have survived, for they are strung out at intervals along the pathway. As you dip downhill you will see a large field in front and, on the skyline slightly to the right, a patch of woodland. That is Blackberry Fox Covert.

The bridleway to Great Harrowden is well trodden. It skirts the big field to the left and then bends right to the skyline. Increasingly the path becomes firmer; in due course it develops into a proper gravel trackway. In the distance, on the skyline in front, are the barns and rooftops of Great Harrowden, half hidden by trees. To the right you look down on the new estates of the Wellingborough suburbs. To the left you can see the tower of Orlingbury church on the horizon. All around the views are extensive, for you are quite high up here.

The gravel trackway leads to the road. To see Great Harrowden, which incidentally, is much smaller than Little Harrowden, turn right. It is dominated by a splendid 18th century Hall.

The circular route continues along a footpath to the right of the Orlingbury road, almost opposite the gate you came through after the gravel trackway from Hardwick. The footpath signpost for the final section points diagonally across the field. Whilst walking that way, aim for the right hand end of the houses on the skyline. Not that there should be any problem. You can see the route clearly ahead. At the bottom of the field, in the distant hedgerow, are a gate, a plank bridge and another gate. Beyond these you follow the side of a field (with the fence on your left) to another gate. Beside a back garden the path leads on to become a track and then a lane. You emerge nearly opposite Little Harrowden church. Turn left to return to the Lamb Inn.

Little Harrowden church is a sad building: an ancient church without a tower. That became unsafe and had to be demolished in 1967. A pity, for it had been a Norman tower. The rest of the building is 14th century. It may interest the energetic that the footpath leading up beside the church goes to Orlingbury. But the return from there would have to be made by road.

Castle Ashby
The Falcon

Strictly speaking this is a hotel with pub facilities as opposed to a pub with hotel facilities. Be that as it may, it provides an excellent base for a circular walk.

The Falcon is a sturdy 16th century building, in grey limestone softened by climbing plants, hanging baskets and flowered gardens. There are two separate bars, sympathetically decorated to match the age and ambience of the establishment. In winter, log fires burn in the open grates; in summer, fresh flowers abound. There is a restaurant where menus are ever-changing. But always the food is home-made, using wherever possible fresh local produce. There is a pleasant garden, with lawns and walnut trees. Children and dogs, if well behaved, are welcome.

This is a free house. Real ale is served in the form of Adnams bitter and Hook Norton, and cider is on draught. There is also a wide selection of wines. The Falcon is open normal times.

Telephone: 01604 696200.

How to get there: Castle Ashby stands 8 miles east of Northampton and 3 miles west of Bozeat. It can be reached by country lanes either from the A428 (the villages of Denton and Yardley Hastings having road connections) or from the A45 (turning close to the village of Earls Barton). The Falcon will be found on the northern edge of the village.

Parking: The Falcon has a large car park. Nearby there is also a large public car park where the gravel is surrounded by a grass picnic area. On summer weekends, however, the village can be very busy, especially when some event or other is 'going on' at Castle Ashby House.

Length of the walk: 4 miles. OS Landranger Map 152 Northampton and Milton Keynes (GR: SP 860596).

Castle Ashby is an attractive, unspoilt estate village owned largely – like the House itself – by the Compton family, the Earls of Northampton. All around are the vast and landscaped grounds created by Capability Brown in the 18th century. In the distance are the wooded slopes of Yardley Chase, an ancient hunting forest. The walk offers views over much of this planned countryside where tree avenues, artificial hills and lakes, and rustic vistas delight both eye and mind.

Towards the end of the walk you pass through the village of Whiston, whose church has been described as 'the jewel on a hilltop'. From there, extensive views across the Nene Valley can be enjoyed.

The Walk

From outside the Falcon turn left along the road signposted to Denton and Yardley Hastings. This passes some attractive stone houses on the right and the Castle Ashby farm shop on the left (where teas are served as well as country produce and crafts). Where the road bends to the right, walk through the gate on the left into a pasture field. Strike diagonally across this to the far corner from where you proceed across the next field, also diagonally. This second field is arable so the walk may be slightly difficult depending on the time of year.

The point where you reach a stile onto the Yardley Hastings road is very close to the spectacular avenue of trees which leads up to the Castle (to the left). Southwards it extends to the main A428 road from Northampton to Bedford, and beyond into the Yardley Chase countryside. In all, this avenue is two miles long. You are not allowed to walk down it (it is reserved for Castle visitors only) but you can admire the whole length from this point.

From the avenue turn right, over the cattle grid and up the lane back to the Denton road. There, at a T junction, you turn left and then, shortly afterwards, right down a cul-de-sac signposted to Chadstone.

This is a pleasant, well-shaded little lane that passes some pretty stone cottages and a farming hamlet. Where the lane ends, beyond the buildings, a gravel track leads straight on through a field. This turns right towards a farm (which you see across the field diagonally). When you reach this farm turn left and take the bridleway which leads gently uphill. There are now large fields to your left and a hedgerow to your right. Bearing to the right this pathway soon comes to a small woodland, through which it proceeds to wind around. This stretch, amongst the bushes and undergrowth and sheltered by the trees, can be a trifle muddy.

At the far side of the wood another large field opens out. Follow the side of this, with the hedge to your right. Soon you will be dipping downhill to the road that runs from Whiston to Denton. Cross straight over this road and continue along the bridleway – a signpost points the way. This takes you down towards a little valley. There is no hedgerow here, the track merely runs between two fields. No doubt there would have been a hedgerow once, before the Government started to encourage the enlargement of fields back in the 1960s. As you approach the trees and thicket running along the valley bottom, you will notice that the track bears right, to follow the bottom of the field to your right. This is not how the Ordnance Survey map shows the lie of the land. According to that, the bridleway continues into the thicket and over a bridge. Not that it matters too much, you still reach the same gravel trackway eventually.

Having followed the valley bottom for a short distance, with the field rising up to your right, you meet the gravel trackway at an angle. Back to your left is a ford, with the elusive bridge somewhere behind. You walk the other way – to the right. This brings you to the Whiston-Castle Ashby road. You can now see Whiston church ahead, rising up above the fields opposite. Turn left down the road to the village of Whiston (where you have to take a side turning to the right to reach the village proper). The splendid church standing high above the village, is 16th century and boasts one of the finest towers in Northamptonshire. The whole building was constructed in just a few years – a remarkable feat for a church. It was financed by Anthony Catesby, who owned the estate in the early 16th century. He was a member of the famous Catesby family, of Gunpowder Plot connections.

To reach the church (and to continue the circular walk) you must leave the village street to the right. A gate in the corner leads to a path which runs uphill between a barn on the left and a tall hedge on the right. Continue on through the churchyard, to a stile on the far side. In fact, it is not exactly a stile. It is a gap in the wall with three horizontal iron rods. Over this you turn right to walk along the side

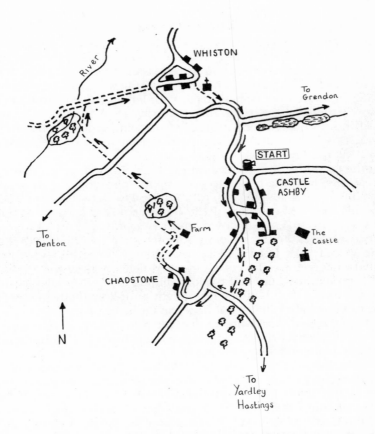

WHISTON

To
Grendon

START

CASTLE
ASHBY

The
Castle

To
Denton

Farm

CHADSTONE

N

To
Yardley
Hastings

River

of a field, with the hedge on your right. At the top a gap leads into the next field. Here you continue in the same direction: a double-rutted track of grass and stones leads up between two fields. No hedgerow here, but there are some excellent views all round. Looking back you will see Whiston church perched on its hill, with the Nene valley beyond.

Very soon you are back on the road. Turn left. The last half mile back to Castle Ashby is along the road. But it is not a busy road and the scenery is pleasant. If you have time you could make a detour to the left, along the road to Grendon. A short way along there, on the right, are the ornamental lakes of the Castle Ashby estate. This is a pleasant spot, where many people come to enjoy the waterside walks and picnic on the tables provided.

Rushton
The Thornhill Arms

This attractive and quiet little pub is older inside than it looks from the outside. It is 300 years old and boasts flagstone floors, stone walls, real beams and open fires. The two bars are comfortable and old-worldly and the atmosphere is restrained and friendly. The garden, which is to the side of the building, looks out over the cricket pitch.

It is a free house, serving various real ales including Ruddles, Bateman and Webster's. But it is the food here that makes the Thornhill Arms special. There is a wide choice, from simple snacks to light meals to full three-course efforts. A small blackboard on the bar lists the burgers available, a large 'whiteboard' on the wall lists the main courses – curry, steak, gammon, cod. Pasta and rice are served as well as the ubiquitous chips. Starters and desserts vary from day to day. The pub keeps normal opening times. The entrance to the bars is at the rear of the building, reached from the car park. Children are welcome, but you should stop them talking to any strangers – the pub is said to be haunted!

Telephone: 01536 710251.

How to get there: Rushton will be found in the countryside between Corby and Kettering. It can be reached either from the A6003 road which runs between those two towns, or else from the smaller towns of Rothwell and Desborough, which stand to the west of the village. The Thornhill Arms faces the church.

Parking: There is a car park at the rear of the Thornhill Arms. Vehicles can also be left on the roadside in the village streets.

Length of the walk: 4½ miles. OS Landranger Map 141 Kettering and Corby (GR: SP 843829).

The walk is an easy one to follow. It offers extensive views across northern Northamptonshire and will satisfy both wild flower enthusiasts and bird watchers. The countryside is unspoilt: there is little to suggest that, here, you are almost surrounded by towns – Corby, Kettering, Desborough and Rothwell.

The Walk
Rushton is a pleasant little village and well worth a tour before setting off on the walk. The path to Pipewell, being a bridleway, is clearly marked the whole way and should not present any difficulties. It starts almost opposite the Thornhill Arms, next to an old stone barn. The sign here points up a wide grassy track. This runs past an old farmyard on the left and, a little further on, a row of cottages on the right. Soon after these you cross over the railway line (here set within a deep cutting) and into the open countryside. You may like to linger here a while, leaning on the brick parapet and watching the wildlife – and occasional train – go by.

The track can be seen ahead of you, running up and down in a fairly straight line. It is double-rutted, grassy and dry since the ground underfoot is stony and hard. To the left is a long hedgerow, dotted with trees; to the right are the open fields. And as the track rises to the near horizon so the views all around open out.

In due course, after about a mile, the track begins its long gradual descent into Pipewell. The hedgerow to your left stops but another, this time to your right, starts. Now the open fields, and the views, are to the west towards Market Harborough. Soon you will find yourself aiming to the right of a cottage, brick-built, gabled and probably Edwardian in date. The track passes under a line of pylons (what an ugly excrescence!) and then suddenly narrows, squeezing itself between houses and gardens down to the road. This last section – some 100 yards in length – can be a trifle muddy, especially after wet weather and the churning of horses' hooves. And the trees above, lovely as they are, prevent the sun from penetrating. Once on the

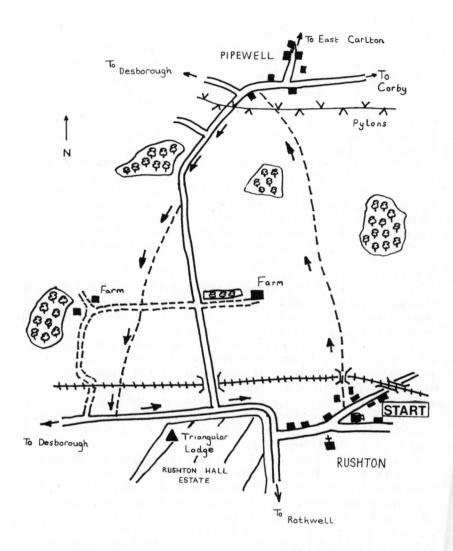

tarmac of the Corby-Desborough road, you will find yourself opposite an attractive Victorian gothic lodge house – one of the entrances to the Pipewell estate.

Pipewell village (pronounced 'Pipwell') will be found by turning right then left. It is really little more than a hamlet – a string of stone-built cottages and, at the far end and just round the corner, a tiny church which looks more like a folly. But there are some magnificent trees here and almost every garden looks as though it has been created by an expert. A lovely spot – and interesting too. For it is here, in the fields on either side, that you can see the remnants of a once great monastery. Across the pastures – especially visible when the sun is low in the sky – are the tell-tale signs of former habitation. Humps and bumps, grassy embankments and hollows, ridges, hillocks and ponds – all these mark out the foundations of a Cistercian abbey. The monastic buildings themselves, together with their associated manors, farms and cottages, must have covered a vast area indeed. At one time, in the Middle Ages, this was one of the richest and most powerful monasteries in southern England.

The return to Rushton begins along the road signposted to Kettering, starting near the gothic lodge house mentioned above. After about ½ mile you pass, on the right, a lane 'unsuitable for heavy goods vehicles', closely followed by a belt of woodland. Shortly after this, and just before a farm on the left (Town's Close Lodge), you take a footpath on the right signposted to Rothwell. Over a rickety stile you will find yourself in a great field. Bear half left and cross this field diagonally, aiming for the left hand edge of a distant woodland. In the following field you walk along the right hand side of a hedgerow, this path bringing you onto a gravel lane. From here the footpath continues straight ahead (across the lane where it rounds a double bend). On the skyline you will see the Rothwell water tower. Keep this in sight, ahead but slightly to the left, as you walk across the field in front of you. The alignment is clearly marked. This eventually brings you to the railway line, which you cross to the right of a cutting, and then (across another field) to the Rushton-Desborough road. If the conditions are very wet you could, if you wish, follow the gravel lane itself, westwards to Gaultney Wood and then south to the road, passing under the railway line.

Once on the road turn left. Soon you will reach, on the right hand side and behind a stone wall, the Triangular Lodge. This was built in the late 16th century by Sir Thomas Tresham (father of Francis, the Gunpowder Plotter) who – as a convert to Roman Catholicism – had an obsession with the Trinity. Accordingly, this folly, built at the corner of his estate, was given three of everything – sides, roofs, floors – or multiples of three – windows, decorations and so on. A strange edifice indeed! It is now owned by English Heritage.

There is a legend that a secret tunnel links the Triangular Lodge with Rushton Hall. You could look for it if you wish. But you might prefer to take the easier way back: along the pavement which accompanies the estate boundary wall all the way back to the village. At least the Thornhill Arms is no legend.

Brigstock
The Green Dragon

A very apt name this, since the pub is now run by a Chinese family who cook a full Eastern menu. The Green Dragon is an old stone-built inn located on the main village square. Inside, the decoration is traditional with oak beams (much hung with horse brasses) settle-type seating and, round the walls, numerous old prints. There is only one bar but this is subdivided into sections – at one end is the pool table, and up a short flight of steps is a lounge-type room.

It is a Charles Wells pub, serving Broadside and Riding ales as well as Eagle Bitter, draught ciders (including Scrumpy Jack) and various wines. But what makes the Green Dragon unique is the food offered. The menu on the bar is a Chinese take-away menu, so the pub not only feeds customers but also offers a home-eating service. Apart from the usual chop suey, chow mein, sweet-and-sour dishes, there are curry meals, Indonesian specialities and various omelettes.

The Green Dragon is open normal hours every day except Saturday, when it is open all day. Children are welcome but dogs must be kept to the gardens at the rear. The pub is popular with the locals and is gaining something of a reputation for its un-publike food.

Telephone: 01536 373627.

How to get there: Brigstock will be found just 4 miles south-east of Corby, on the A6116 road to Thrapston. The main road, in fact, now bypasses the village on its eastern side. The Green Dragon stands on the old main road, on the left hand side as you come from Corby. It faces the village square and central medieval cross.

Parking: The Green Dragon has a car park. Vehicles can also be left at the roadside in many of the village side streets. The central square (more like a triangle) is not busy and cars can also be left there.

Length of the walk: 5 miles. OS Landranger Map 141 Kettering and Corby (GR: SP 946854).

This walk offers three types of scenery: farmland, woodland and landscaped parkland. It also passes a mansion (Fermyn Woods Hall) and the Bocase Stone, a historic marker stone steeped in legend and myth. Throughout, the route is clearly signposted, with footpath arrow discs nailed to stiles and wooden posts. The stretches through woodlands can be muddy and so good walking shoes are recommended.

The Walk

Take the road which runs behind the Green Dragon until you reach a footpath signpost on your left (about 200 yards distant, just before a row of houses). From the stile here the path leads along the edge of a field to a stile on the far side. You must now cross the bypass, which along this stretch runs in a cutting. At the other side another signpost points the way. Over several stiles you now follow the edge of three large fields, keeping the hedgerow to your left the whole way. At the bottom end of the third field, at the left hand edge of a large woodland, you will find a stile. This leads over a barbed-wire fence and into a nettle-strewn corner beyond the hedge. Turn right, cross a plank bridge over a ditch and enter the wood. The pathway now becomes very pleasant indeed, if a little muddy. It meanders about amongst the trees and, after turning left, proceeds up a wide forest ride, the tall trees either side forming an avenue. At the far end you reach a gate into a field. Do not go through this. Instead, turn right over some planks which cross the ditches here, and continue through the wood. Soon you come out into the open, with a large arable field ahead. Continue in the same direction, with this field to your right and the woodland to your left. There are some farm buildings over to your right and a stone barn ahead, amongst some trees. Just before the barn turn left over a well-built footbridge. You now continue along the edge of the large field ahead, keeping the hedgerow to your left. At the far side of the next field you reach the Benefield road, close to Lodge Cottages. At this point you are very close to Fermyn Woods

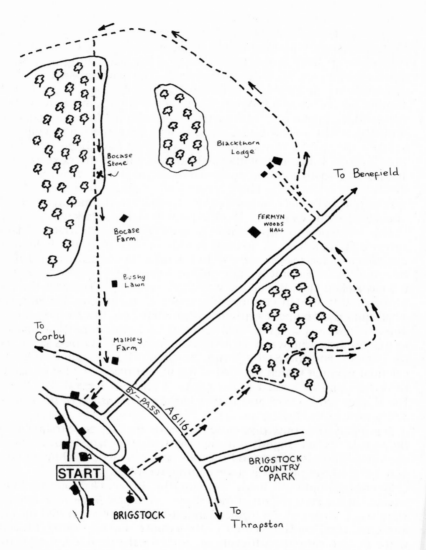

Hall. Indeed if you walk down the road to your left you will be able to see the mansion across the fields. It is a handsome building but little remains of its origins as a 14th century hunting lodge. It has been enlarged, renovated and altered over the centuries and today is largely a Victorian and Edwardian creation.

From Lodge Cottages turn up the road to the right and, after a couple of hundred yards, turn left along the drive to Blackthorn Lodge. It is a dead straight drive and you can see Blackthorn Lodge in front. However, you do not walk all the way up to the Lodge (a stone farmhouse in fact). About two thirds of the way along a footpath marker points the way off to the right. The path crosses the field diagonally to the edge of a belt of woodland. Beyond, it passes into another field. Now you turn left. Keeping the open arable field to your right and the hedgerow to your left, you continue in a fairly straight direction. Over a footbridge into the next field, the path eventually bears to the left, to run behind the hedge you have been following. Now it is on your right, with a field to the left. At the next gateway are more footpath and bridleway marker signs. Here turn left and walk towards the woodland. There a gate leads through to a grassy track, hemmed in by hedgerow either side. To the left, through the bushes, you will see an open field. To the right is Harry's Park Wood.

The way back to Brigstock is now very clear. The track runs in almost a straight line. At first it is muddy underfoot – not helped by the effect of horses' hooves – but soon it becomes dry and firm. Beyond Bocase Farm it is a gravel lane, beyond Bushy Lawn Lodge it is a tarmacked lane. But all the way there is interest. Towards the end of the muddy stretch you may like to search for the Bocase Stone – a half-buried monument marking the site of the old Bocase Tree. Some people think this was the meeting place of forest archers, who used to practise here (the word deriving from 'bow-cast'). Others say it was the site of ancient Saxon court hearings, 'Bocas' being a Saxon calendar event at which the lord of the manor read out a list of names of those claiming annual forest rights. There is a legend that Robin Hood once hid his bow and arrows in the hollow trunk of the Bocase Tree, whilst evading capture.

Eventually the route dips down towards the bypass. Straight over the bypass (in fact, slightly left then right) another lane leads down to the village and a look around Brigstock would be worth while on your way back to the pub. It is a very attractive place.

Mention should be made here of the Brigstock Country Park, situated at the eastern end of the village, on the far side of the bypass. Here some 40 acres of a former sandpit have been converted into an attractive rural enclave geared to the country-loving visitor. Indeed, there are two car parks officially set aside for the disabled, such is the desire of Northamptonshire County Council to encourage everyone, without exception, to enjoy the countryside.

Woodford
The Dukes Arms

Up to the 19th century this was called the Lords Arms after the Lord of the Manor. The name was changed in honour of the Duke of Wellington who used to come here for a drink whilst visiting his friend Charles Arbuthnot at Woodford House nearby. It is thought to be the oldest public house in the village, dating back at least to the 17th century. The Dukes Arms is an attractive building facing the village green. There are gardens at the back and inside it has a bar, a lounge and separate games room for pool, skittles and darts. The decor has been designed with sympathy for the age of the building and is comfortable and old-fashioned. Children are welcome but not dogs owing to the serving of food.

It is a Courage house and has a wide range of real ales, including Ruddles. Cider is on draught. Food is always available. Specialities of the house include home-made meat pies and desserts made with liqueurs (delicious!) The pub is open normal times, and there is access for the disabled.

Telephone: 01832 732224.

How to get there: Woodford is located just south of the A14, the A1-M1 link road. It is a little to the west of Thrapston and 6 miles east of Kettering. From the A14 it can be reached either by the Thrapston/Corby turn-off or the Finedon – Wellingborough turn-off. The Dukes Arms will be found on the left as you enter the village centre from the north.

Parking: The pub has a car park. There is no public car park in Woodford but there is ample space for roadside parking throughout the village.

Length of the walk: 4 miles. OS Landranger Map 141 Kettering and Corby (GR: SP 967770).

This walk is not so much circular as a figure '8' shape. It goes to the village of Denford and back, across the Nene Valley, passing through some varied scenery (riverside water-meadows, upland farmlands and woodlands) and is easily followed. The paths are all clearly marked and signposted.

There are good views throughout the walk and plenty to see for the naturalist. It would suit those intending to linger awhile and enjoy the beauty of this part of Northamptonshire at their leisure.

The Walk

The route to Denford follows the Nene Way and is, in consequence, well signposted. Indeed, there is a Nene Way finger post outside the Dukes Arms. The Way runs for a distance of 70 miles, from Badby in the west of the county to Wansford in the north-east corner of the county. It links various rights of way, paths and bridleways and was instigated by Northamptonshire County Council. It was officially opened in 1990 and has proved very popular with walkers. The stretch from Woodford to Denford is fairly direct and runs for less then 2 miles. Visitors to this area may be interested to learn that hereabouts runs a dialectal dividing line. Upstream from here – that is south towards Northampton – locals pronounce the river the 'Nen' whilst downstream – towards Cambridgeshire and the Fens – it is more commonly called the 'Neen'.

Walking downhill from the Dukes Arms, passing the White Horse Inn on your left, you have a pleasant view straight ahead over the Nene Valley. At the bottom of the road is a T junction. To the right is the church, to the left (the direction you take) the lane passes some old cottages and a farm and heads out towards the open countryside. At the cattle grid, notice the attractive, old-fashioned looking cottage on your right; remarkably, it is a new building.

A little way along the path, as it makes its way over a field towards some woodland, you will see a stile on your left marked 'Nene Way'. Turn to the right here and head across the field – the path is clear – directly towards Denford church spire in the distance. Between this path and the woods to your left, incidentally, are the terraced remnants of the old Dower House and gardens owned by Lord St. John. They were erased from the landscape in the early 19th century and, today, you need to be an archaeologist fully to appreciate the irregularities in the ground. Hereabouts, many people like to set down their picnics, such are the splendid views over the Nene meadows.

By way of fields and gates the path descends to the river itself, to follow its northern bank. There are willows along this stretch, water-loving wild flowers and, on the Nene, passing boat traffic. A lovely scene to be sure. Soon you come to a sluice gate, controlling the river flow, and then the line of a dismantled railway. Through the gate – the Nene Way is still well marked – you strike across the field in front, keeping Denford church directly ahead. The route, now, is flat and straight, passing through fields and gates. After the last gate however – with the final big field in front – you bear left and keep to the line of the hedgerow. This leads directly to the bridge over the river. In fact, there are several bridges here since the Nene divides at this point. A lock can be seen to the left and, to the right, the workings connected with the 'siphonic weir' (which regulates river flow). Denford stands immediately opposite and you may wish to walk across and have a look round. It is a bustling place with an interesting 14th century church. A jumble of lanes lead off from the winding main street, now much quieter since the bypass was finished.

The return route is more circuitous than the outward journey. Turn left after recrossing the bridges (having been in to the village) and follow the river bank. There is a broad sweep of a meander here and you can walk along the raised levee, past the anglers. The path is clear and, keeping the river to your left, you cannot go wrong. Soon you find yourself back at the dismantled railway, quickly followed by the sluice gate. But now, instead of going through the gate marked Nene Way you strike uphill to the right. Head for the skyline, where you will find a gate and stile in the top corner of the field. Through here a clear track leads to Woodford Grange, a large block of stone cottages. Just before these turn left (slightly back on yourself) and walk towards the higher end of the field. Soon this path becomes a clear track again, passing through a double farm gate. Straight on and another gate will be found. Beyond this the path heads straight for a patch of woodland in front. To the right a view opens up – unfortunately across countryside now disfigured by the A14 dual carriageway.

The track curves round into the woodland. This is called Woodford Shrubbery. Years ago it was called Stone Pit Common and was a

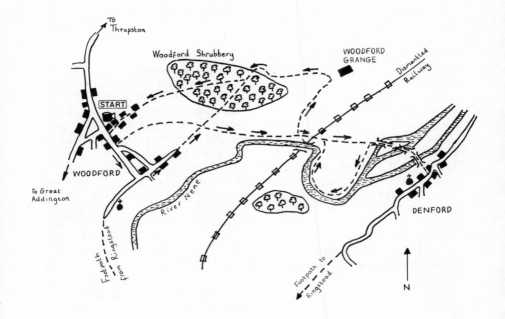

favourite meeting place for local ironstone workers. They used to gather here for secret drinking sessions, away from the prying eyes of wives and employers. Today the area is quiet and rich in wildlife of a different variety! There is a clear trackway through the woods but you do not stay on it for long. After just 100 yards or so you strike off to the right through an offset gate-opening. Through this a smaller path winds its way through the trees. You soon come out into a field, on the far side of which is Whittlesea Terrace. This, running through a small housing estate, leads back to Woodford village green and the inn.

Now, if you have the time and inclination, you can visit the church. It has a wealth of interest – Norman architectural features, ornate memorials and – most famous of all – a human heart. You will find it behind a glass panel in one of the pillars of the nave. It is shrivelled and dry but still recognisably heart-shaped. No-one knows for sure how old it is or who it once belonged to. One theory is that it is the heart of a lord of the manor who died in 1290 during one of the Crusades. Another theory says it belonged to a 16th century vicar who converted to Roman Catholicism and subsequently fled to Belgium taking the valuable church chalice with him. Either way, the heart is ancient indeed.

Wadenhoe
The King's Head

This is an attractive 17th century pub which has benefited from not being refurbished, renovated or rebuilt over recent years. It is an ordinary village pub in the best sense – there are no frills and no fussy tourist-geared facilities. There are bare stone walls, old tiled floors, sparse decoration and simple seating in the form of benches and stools. It is a locals' pub. However, there is one feature which makes the King's Head a particular favourite amongst walkers and other visitors. This is the garden. The lawns stretch down to the riverbank and wooden tables are set out over the grass – ideal for children. The pub has its own moorings, for this stretch of the Nene is much travelled by narrow boats and river craft. It is a delightful spot.

The King's Head is a free house serving various real ales including Marston's Pedigree, Bateman and Greene King. A limited range of food is offered, the daily menu being written up on a blackboard in the public bar. Chiefly this consists of ploughman's lunches, sandwiches and simple chip-based 'basket' meals. Normal pub opening times are kept.

Telephone: 018015 222.

How to get there: Wadenhoe is located towards the eastern end of the county, 3 miles south-west of Oundle and 4 miles north of Thrapston. It is most easily reached from the A605 road which runs between those two towns, taking the turning at Thorpe Waterville and going through Aldwincle. The King's Head stands at the southern end of the village, down the bottom of the cul-de-sac that leads to the church.

Parking: There is a car park at the pub. Vehicles can also be left at the roadside along the village streets.

Length of the walk: 3½ miles. OS Landranger Map 141 Kettering and Corby (GR: TL 011834).

Wadenhoe is a very popular centre for walking: there are many footpaths radiating out from the village and there is some lovely unspoilt countryside all around. This circular walk runs from Wadenhoe to Aldwincle, both very attractive villages with some historic interest, and back. The outward journey follows the Nene Way — that long distance footpath which the County Council has designated from Badby to Wansford, winding along the course of the river Nene. The return jouney is through open farmland (sturdy footwear advisable) and, for a short stretch, along the line of a medieval road. The paths used are clearly marked throughout, with numerous signposts and directional arrow discs nailed to gates or to the many stiles.

The Walk

From outside the King's Head walk down to the gate at the end of the road, where stands a footpath signpost and a Nene Way indicator. From here there is a good view up to the church, standing on a knoll to your half-right. The path you take, however, is not the one that leads up to the church. You will be returning down that at the end of the walk. Instead you keep to the lower land, below the church which you pass to your right. The path leads through some woodland, keeping fairly close to the river Nene on your left. There are many Nene Way marker posts along this stretch and so a detailed description of the route should not be necessary. Suffice it to say that this is a most pleasant walk. The path meanders through the trees and, here and there, are glimpses of the river. The land slopes down to the bank and care should be taken when conditions are muddy.

Soon you reach an open field, along the side of which the path continues, keeping the trees to your left. As you rise up above the meadows so a view opens out to your left, towards Achurch, whose spire you can see above the distant trees. After crossing a footbridge the path goes uphill, to run along the ends of the long gardens of Aldwincle village, over the wall to your right. The river Nene can be

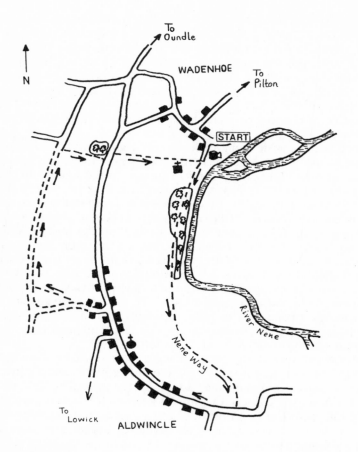

seen winding its way into the distance down to your left. When level
with Aldwincle's spired church you bear left, across a field towards
the tower of Aldwincle's other church. Crossing the corner of the next
field, and over two stiles, you aim to the right of a clump of trees.
Another stile there leads to the road. If you turn left you will come to
the now redundant All Saints' church. This dates from the 13th
century and boasts a wonderfully ornate tower. Opposite this is the
former rectory (now a private residence) where John Dryden was
born in 1631. He became the Poet Laureate under Charles II despite
having supported Cromwell during the Civil War.

To continue the circular walk, turn right after meeting the road
from the Nene Way and continue through the village. Past St. Peter's
church on your right (note the tall broach spire) you turn left down

Cross Lane. This is a dead end for vehicular traffic, for it soon becomes a gravel track, but is a public right of way for walkers. If the ground is very wet it might be advisable now to continue along this trackway, to a T junction where you turn right. Otherwise you can take the footpath over the fields. You will see the signpost to your right just beyond the last of the houses. The path leads fairly straight, across four fields, all the while keeping the hedgerow to your right. There is a stile to climb, and two plank bridges to cross. But the walk is very easy.

When you meet the main trackway turn right. This is a wide, grassy-muddy route, with hedgerows either side some five yards apart. It is of ancient origin and once formed a section of the road from Oundle to Thrapston, which followed the western side of the Nene valley. It was first created, probably, by the Saxons who did not wish to use the Roman road on the other side of the valley (a course now followed by the A605 road). It continued in use throughout the Middle Ages and into the days of coach travel. Decline set in after the Industrial Revolution. Today most of the route is a country lane. But the section from Wadenhoe to Lowick – this stretch you are now following – is just a wide track, used only by tractors and horses. In due course you meet the tarmac of a metalled road. To the left a private lane leads to Aldwincle Lodge. At this point you turn right down the side of a large field keeping the hedgerow to your left. This path takes you to the Wadenhoe-Aldwincle road. Turn left.

Just a short way along you will see a clear track to your right. A signpost tells you that it leads to Wadenhoe church, and a cattle grid takes you across to a gravelled, double-rutted path. The field to your right is often used for scout camps. Wadenhoe church is perched on a little hill, with trees on one side, and views across the Nene on the other. It is a splendid sight. The saddle-back tower is Norman in origin, although some of the church foundations are believed to be Saxon. The earthworks in the field to the north (to your left) indicate the site of an early settlement. So this whole area is steeped in history – literally.

The path that leads down from the church takes you to the gate that marked the start of the walk. Once again, you will find yourself on the Nene meadows. You may now have time to enjoy, again, the busy scene: the river traffic, the rustling of the trees and the active snipe.

Barnwell
The Montagu Arms

This pub is named after the family of the Duke of Gloucester who lives at nearby Barnwell Castle. The link is this – his father was the third son of King George V who was created a Duke in 1928 and married, in 1935, Lady Alice Montagu-Douglas-Scott, daughter of the 7th Duke of Buccleuch (owner of Boughton House near Kettering). The present Duke, Richard, was the second son of that marriage. The Montagu Arms is a lovely old building with low ceilings and oak beams. It has been renovated and extended over recent years, to accommodate extra hotel facilities and a new lounge bar, but still the traditional character has been retained. The main bar has bare stonework and much woodwork on display.

It is a free house serving a range of real ales including Greene King, Bateman and Hook Norton. Draught cider and many selected wines are also offered. All the food is home-made, with fresh local vegetables used wherever possible. The usual pub fare is provided – pies, sausages, fish, salads and various cold snacks. Normal opening times are observed.

Children are not just welcome but positively encouraged by the extensive play area in the gardens behind. Dogs, however, are less happily tolerated.

Telephone: 01832 273726.

How to get there: Barnwell is situated just 3 miles south of Oundle, a little to the east of the A605 road to Thrapston. The Montagu Arms stands at the northern end of the village, at the corner of the road to Thurning.

Parking: There is a car park at the pub and plenty of space along the village streets where vehicles may be left at the roadside.

Length of the walk: 4 miles. OS Landranger Map 141 Kettering and Corby and 142 Peterborough (GR: TL 050849). Barnwell will be found on the very edge of each of these two sheets.

The walk crosses some of the pleasant and unspoilt countryside to the south of the pretty village of Barnwell. It is an easy, well-marked route with clear paths and flat terrain. The last stretch follows the course of the Nene Way, the long distance footpath designated by the County Council which runs almost the entire length of Northamptonshire. The section included here runs alongside a deserted railway track and over a disused level crossing. It ends at All Saints' church in the village, now a ruin with only the chancel remaining.

The Walk

Barnwell is a long, narrow settlement with two lines of cottages facing each other across a small stream. There is a ford half way along and many footbridges connect the two parallel lanes. The buildings represent almost every age and style of architecture from medieval thatched cottages to modern bungalows, via Georgian and Victorian residences. The gardens are well kept and everything seems to be in the dappled shade of majestic trees. This was an important settlement back in the Middle Ages. It was divided into two parishes (All Saints and St. Andrews, the latter still being the main church) and was once described as a 'considerable town'. It held a weekly market, an annual fair, an assize of bread and ale and had seven wells used for 'miracle cures of baby illnesses'. Decline set in during the 18th century when the place depopulated and the farmland all around was enclosed for sheep grazing.

From the Montagu Arms you walk up the left hand lane through the village, keeping the stream to your right. After passing all the houses and cottages this lane becomes a gravel track and continues in the same direction. Once in open countryside you will find yourself overlooking a low-lying field, with embankments all round and a dam-like structure going away to your right. If you think it looks like a dried out reservoir you would almost be correct. It is, in fact, a flood storage reservoir. It controls water flow during wet weather and can fill up when necessary, thus preventing Barnwell village being flooded. The gravel track continues straight on, with this empty reservoir to your right. At the end of this section that track turns sharply left and a wide open field presents itself in front of you. Although not signposted, the footpath leads over this field, slightly to the left of straight on.

This is a very easy walk, taking you across the arable fields and over a bridge. Straight on still you begin to rise towards the trees dotted along the skyline. In less than ½ mile you reach a stony trackway. If you turn left you would reach Clopton village, close to the county

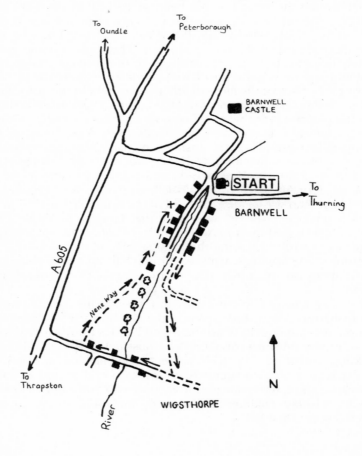

boundary. By turning right, however, you come to the hamlet of Wigsthorpe. By this time the track has become a metalled lane. Wigsthorpe is an attractive little place – some old stone cottages and a couple of farms. At the far end, to the right and just beyond Wigsthorpe Farm Cottage, you will see a signpost marking the Nene Way. The bridleway – for such the path is, along the next stretch of the Way – leads along the side of a field with the garden to your right. At the end of the garden you strike across the field ahead, aiming for a break in the distant hedge where the bridleway passes through.

The next field is another very large one. Again, walk straight across. The line of trees over to your right follows the route of a disused railway line – one that came up from Irthlingborough, via Thrapston, and went on to Oundle and Wansford. From Wansford to Peterborough the same line has been preserved, as the Nene Valley Railway. The bridleway meets this old railway line where the trees end. Here is an interesting little Victorian building, once the workplace of a level crossing attendant. The level crossing itself, of course, has gone but it is not hard to picture the scene 100 years ago.

From here the way back to Barnwell village is fairly direct. It runs across to the back of the farm and then along behind the houses of the village. In due course you reach a kissing gate. This leads you through into the old graveyard which surrounds All Saints' church. Only the chancel remains. The rest of the building was demolished in 1825, having fallen into disrepair. Inside are many Montagu memorials, including one commemorating Henry Montagu, who drowned in a pond in 1625 (at just 3 years old), and another in memory of John Montagu, Fourth Earl of Sandwich. He was the gambler and spendthrift who was made First Lord of the Admiralty in 1771 in Lord North's government. He was also the famous inventor of the sandwich: a slice of meat between two slices of bread was a snack he could enjoy without leaving the gaming table.

Return to the Montagu Arms by turning left out of the churchyard, and walking on the other side of the stream from your outward journey.

For those having to push prams and wheelchairs, combining your visit to Barnwell with time spent at the Country Park cannot be too strongly recommended. It will be found 2 miles northwards, close to the southern outskirts of Oundle. Constructed out of old gravel workings, and opened in 1971, it offers varied facilities over a 37 acre site. Around a warden-attended information centre and toilets are landscaped lakes, waterside meadows, and walks through wildlife-rich habitats. Fishing facilities are offered, including those especially geared for the disabled.

Wakerley
The Exeter Arms

Down in the meadows below the village was once an ancient manor house. It was the home of the Cecil family before Burghley House was built near Stamford. And that is why this pub has such a name: the Cecils became the Marquises of Exeter.

The Exeter Arms is a large handsome building which hides the fact that it goes back 300 years. It has obviously been much altered and expanded – especially during the 19th century. Be that as it may, the interior is decidedly homely and comfortable, the oak beams and old sporting prints on the walls helping to give the place character. The pub is reputedly haunted so be careful who you speak to in that dark corner!

It is a free house, serving selected beers including Bateman and Adnams Broadside. Strongbow is the draught cider offered. A wide choice of food is available every day except Monday. Apart from the regular menu – which includes home-made pies, lasagne, curry, chicken and other such typical pub fare – daily specials are listed on the blackboard next to the bar. Rolls and sandwiches are also available. Normal opening times are kept. Inside there is one main room with a central bar and dining area, together with a games room beyond. Outside there is a lawn with tables and – for the children – swings. Indeed children are welcome inside as well, as are pet dogs. Telephone: 01572 87817.

How to get there: Wakerley is situated very close to the Leicestershire border, just 6 miles south-west of Stamford and 8 miles north-east of Corby. It can be reached down a side road from the main A43 road close to Duddington. The Exeter Arms stands at the eastern end of the village, below the church which sits on the hillslope behind.

Parking: There is a car park in front of the pub and an overflow one to the side. Vehicles can also be left at the roadside along the village street.

Length of the walk: 2½ miles. OS Landranger Map 141 Kettering and Corby (GR: SP 955995).

Wakerley Great Wood, which stretches across the area south of the village, is owned by the Forestry Commission. Over recent years it has been opened up to the public and is now a very popular centre for walking, riding, picnicking and nature study. Forest trails have been laid out, and many miles of bridleways (stout footwear advisable if you are walking on these). There are also narrow paths and grassy rides through the trees. Walkers are allowed over all of them, and so can devise their own circular walks. Children will enjoy exploring, and will learn much about nature from the labels dotted around which identify tree species. Some of the 'official' trackways are firm and dry, with sand or gravel surfaces. These are suitable for prams and wheelchairs.

Walkers are asked to remember that pheasant shooting takes place between 30th September and 30th January, although this is carefully regulated. Deer shooting is also necessary sometimes as too many deer can seriously damage the plant life of the forest.

This circular walk should be seen only as a suggested route, following neither the 'Red Trail' (1½ miles) nor the 'Blue Trail' (1 mile), both 'official' marked routes. You will get the feel of Wakerley Wood and can have an excellent view of Laxton Hall.

The Walk

For those wishing to start the walk from the Exeter Arms there is a footpath which leads uphill, passing the church, to the edge of Wakerley Great Wood. The walk can also start at the Forestry Commission car park. In case you get lost amongst the trees, you should remember that a wide sand-and-gravel track – indeed, a main forest thoroughfare – runs up the middle of Wakerley Wood from

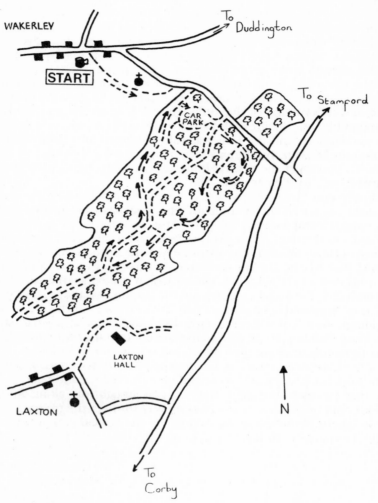

near the entrance to the car park by the road to the south-west corner. This track is set aside for Forestry Commission vehicles, although (of course) walkers are allowed, together with prams and wheelchairs.

From close to the beginning of this main trackway you take the path to the left, marked by a red band around a wooden post. This is the start of the official 'Red' route. It curves round and crosses a bridleway along which riders need a permit giving them access. There are signs which indicate such a bridleway. On the second occasion that you meet this bridleway you turn left to follow it, thus leaving the Red route. You now keep to this new path until you eventually meet the main central trackway.

All along this part of the walk you are fairly close to the edge of the woodland. If you have time you should leave the security of the bridleway and strike off to your left through the trees. Your efforts may be rewarded. From certain points along the woodland's southern perimeter you get views of Laxton Hall, a splendid classical mansion, built at the beginning of the 19th century. It is private and not open to the public but the grounds can be enjoyed from afar. It is said that the parkland around the Hall was fully designed and landscaped by Humphrey Repton, but he was never paid for his trouble.

When you meet the central trackway you turn right, to begin the journey back to the car park.

Should you turn left, instead, you will eventually reach the south-western corner of the woodland. This end has only been forested since the last war for it covers part of the area once used as a wartime airfield. On this site, and across the farmland to the west, towards the village of Harringworth, was Spanhoe Airfield, used during the Second World War by the US 9th Air Force. It was from runways here that Dakotas flew out, towing the gliders which played such a part in the Arnhem raid, the Rhine crossing and the landings on the D Day beach-heads in Normandy. Today you may still see some of the old service buildings, now converted to farm use. And there is a small stone memorial standing at the side of the road between Laxton village and Harringworth, marking the end of one of the old runways.

Back on the main trackway heading north-eastwards (having turned right from the bridleway), you continue until the second bend – the one that curves to the right. Here you go straight on, along another permit-only bridleway. This wends its way through the trees, close to the northern perimeter of the Wood. In due course you arrive back at the car park. Turn left to return to the village and the inn.

Kings Cliffe
The Cross Keys Inn

This is a lovely old pub both inside and out, and fully deserves its listing as a building of architectural and historic interest. It stands in the village's conservation area. There has been an inn here since 1732 although the main part of the structure is older than that – probably 17th century. Many additions and alterations have been made over the years and so parts are not easy to date. Much of the rear is 18th century, as are many of the doorways. A few of the windows are 19th century. Some renovations have taken place in recent years. The result of all this is a most interesting interior – with low beams, a maze of rooms, inglenook fireplaces and, in the depths, a vaulted cellar. There is a public bar, and two separate lounges, all decorated with taste. There is no garden but seating is provided outside on a terrace.

The Cross Keys is a free house serving Bass beers. Draught cider comes in the form of Dry Blackthorn. Meals and bar snacks are available every day, lunch and evening, except Sunday evenings. The pub prides itself on its home-made cooking. There is a wide choice of food and no one should go hungry. Normal opening times are kept.

Telephone: 01780 470276.

How to get there: **Kings** Cliffe will be found towards the north-east corner of the county, just 6 miles south of Stamford. Corby is 10 miles away, in a south-westerly direction. The village is not served by a main road. To reach it, you must leave the A43 near Deene Park and travel through the villages of Bulwick and Blatherwycke. Alternatively you could drive down from the A42 Peterborough road from Wittering Airfield. The Cross Keys will be found opposite the church.

Parking: The pub has its own car park. Vehicles can also be parked on the roadside along the village streets. These are not busy.

Length of the walk: 4 miles. OS Landranger Map 141 Kettering and Corby (GR: TL 006972).

This is a very pleasant, easy walk over level countryside to the attractive and unspoilt village of Apethorpe and back. There are no hills to climb, only a few stiles. Throughout, the route is marked by footpath arrow indicators nailed to gates and posts, so there is no excuse to get lost!

The return journey goes past woodland where deer can still be seen. This, perhaps, is only as it should be, since the whole district was once a Royal hunting park.

The Walk

Turning left outside the Cross Keys you walk down the High Street to where it crosses the Willow Brook. There is a bridge here and the river below it babbles along at quite a pace, echoing amongst the trees. Already you feel as though you are in the open countryside. Almost immediately after the river you turn down Morehay Lane on the right, a gravelly, stony track. After just 100 yards or so you come to a footpath signpost, pointing the way off to the left. A pleasant footpath now leads up through the trees, clearly visible but prone to dampness. At the top you come out onto a field. Go straight on, with the fence on your left, to a stile. Over this you continue with the fence on your right. Arrow discs point the way.

Down to the left and in front you will see the ground cut away, gouged out into deep hollows. This is the site of an old clay pit, now mercifully being reclaimed by nature. The path crosses this pit along a raised dyke or embankment, uneven and earthy. Perhaps it was deliberately heaped up by the Council to make the right of way. Without it, the climb down the slope would have been steep and slippery indeed. A stile leads into the next field. On the far side you climb over a double fence – no stile here but obviously an 'official' way through the hedgerow. Beyond, you continue in the same direction with the fence to your left. Soon you arrive at a gravel trackway running across and, to your immediate left, an old barn. An enormous field stretches out in front, with a line of trees on the distant skyline. You walk straight across this field, continuing in the same direction as before. Within the line of bushes and trees ahead you will see a short row of pines. Aim for the right hand end of these.

When you reach that spot you will find a gateway leading through to a gravel road. In fact, there are three roads to choose from here since you emerge at something of a track junction. The gravel road which runs straight on (slightly to the left) is the way to Apethorpe village. The other two are tarmacked country lanes, leading off to the right and sharp right. Each of these is signposted 'Private Road'. The former goes to Apethorpe House Farm. The latter goes to Spa Farm. After looking round Apethorpe village you will return to this spot and take the lane to Spa Farm.

Apethorpe is the quintessential English village in a picturesque valley setting: stone cottages, many of them thatched, grouped around a war memorial, a whipping post and stocks, a 15th century church, and even an old dovecote, although this has been converted into a water tower. It is an estate village, for close by is Apethorpe Hall. This manor house dates back to Tudor times and was once the home of the Mildmay family. Sir Walter Mildmay, who was the first to own it, was Chancellor of the Exchequer under Elizabeth I. The estate later passed to the Earls of Westmorland. The building has undergone many structural changes since it was first constructed but is still magnificent. The landscaped parkland includes a large lake.

The way back to Kings Cliffe is very clear. To begin with, you follow the lane already mentioned to Spa Farm. This is a very pleasant stroll despite being over a metalled surface. There are wide views either side, across arable fields, and you will be very unlucky if even one vehicle passes. In due course the lane leads you through some woods, mainly deciduous on the left and coniferous on the right. You do not actually walk all the way to Spa Farm. Where the lane bends left, at Spa Farm Cottages you go straight on. You will see the stile and footpath arrow against the hedge to your right. The path squeezes itself between a hedgerow on one side and a back garden on the other.

At the end of the back garden is a large field, which you skirt, continuing straight on with the hedgerow to your right. Beyond the next gate you walk through woodland. This is where deer are frequently seen, so walk quietly and keep your eyes peeled. At the far side of the wood you reach an open field again. Walk straight on, keeping the hedgerow to your right. Do the same when you reach the next large field and you will eventually find a gate that leads on to Morehay Lane. Kings Cliffe is now immediately in front of you, and there is an excellent view of the church across the Willow Brook meadows. By turning left and following Morehay Lane round – it is

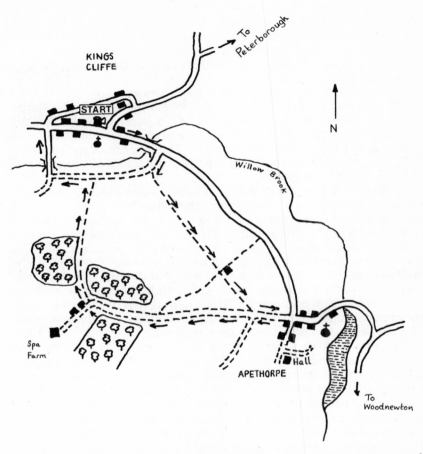

a grassy-gravelly track – you will eventually come to the western end of the High Street. By this route you will be able to see the village in its near-entirety (the Cross Keys being at the eastern end).

Kings Cliffe is a large village, almost entirely stone built. In the Middle Ages it was an important market centre, having three weekly markets and an annual three-day fair. Sadly most of this old settlement was burnt down by avenging Roundheads during the English Civil War, Kings Cliffe having been on the side of the Cavaliers. It is for this reason that few buildings here are older than the 17th century. In more recent times Kings Cliffe was famous for pottery making and wood turning. Indeed, so much wooden ware was made here that the place was once called the 'wooden spoon village'.

Yarwell
The Angel

This is a small country pub of unpretentious character. Inside there are two compact bars and a children's room, all decorated in a simple but traditional style. There are beams, plain walls and a fine stone fireplace housing a woodburning stove. Both children and dogs are welcome and there are gardens at the rear. This is a friendly pub and well-suited to walkers who are both hungry and thirsty.

It is a free house serving Theakston real ale. There is a wide range of food, especially during the summer months when local caravan holidaymakers boost the pub's regular clientele. Apart from the choice in the standard menu, daily specials are written up on the blackboard in the main bar. There are ploughman's lunches and various sandwiches, pizzas, burgers and proper meals, all very reasonably priced. The Angel opens for slightly less than the normal pub hours: daily from 12 noon to 2 pm and 6.30 pm to 11 pm.

Telephone: 01780 782582.

How to get there: Yarwell will be found in the north-east corner of Northamptonshire, close to the border with Cambridgeshire. It is

8 miles west of Peterborough and 5 miles south-east of Stamford. It can be reached from the A47 road, taking the lane from Wansford towards Fotheringhay. The Angel stands in the centre of the village, opposite the church.

Parking: The Angel does not have its own car park. However there is plenty of room in the village for vehicles to be left at the roadside. The village street is wide enough for parked cars not to cause an obstacle.

Length of the walk: 2½ miles. OS Landranger Map 142 Peterborough (GR: TL 069979).

This walk includes the very last stretch of the Nene Way as it leaves the county and heads across Cambridgeshire towards the Wash. There is also a stretch through Old Sulehay Forest, which covers the site of an ancient iron-ore quarry, thought to have been worked originally by the Romans. Today the woodland is rich in flora and fauna and provides excellent walking conditions.

Throughout the circuit the footpaths are clear and well signposted. Two short lengths of road walking are necessary but traffic is light and the views are pleasant.

The Walk

The first ½ mile of this walk is along a road. But it is a quiet road. Turn right outside the Angel and walk through the village to the crossroads at the end. Turn right again, towards Wansford. Fairly soon you will come to a footpath signpost on the left. It points up a wide trackway, bordered on either side by a hedgerow. This leads straight to the woodland, which you can see immediately ahead. As the track reaches the trees it bears half right. In due course you reach a T junction in the wood. There is a gate straight ahead, with a fence either side, and a wide path running across. Turn right. This path is, in fact, a bridleway, and very attractive it is too. Grassy floored and straight-as-a-die it leads under the arch-like branches of tall ash trees. You should not rush along this stretch.

Old Sulehay Forest – for this is the name of the wood – is a dense deciduous woodland where many species of plants can be found. Oak and beech mix with the ash and lime trees, whilst such wild flowers as columbine, anemone and woodruff grow in the rich undergrowth. Many of the trees are coppiced – that is, they have been pruned at ground level to allow for the growth of tall, straight branches. Such a method allowed for the continued supply of timber. Evidently, this woodland was once managed – perhaps to supply a constant quantity of charcoal for local iron-ore smelters. Certainly the limestone hereabouts was once excavated for its iron content. At the edge of

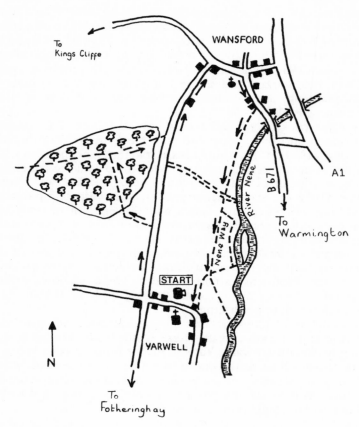

To Kings Cliffe

WANSFORD

A1

River Nene

B 671

To Warmington

Nene Way

START

YARWELL

N

To Fotheringhay

Sulehay Forest the track reaches an iron gate. From here the path continues down the side of a field back to the road. The views ahead are eastwards, towards Peterborough. Surprisingly, however, that city cannot be seen, despite its close proximity.

Turn left along the road and you soon reach the attractive village of Wansford. This was once part of Northamptonshire but is now officially under Cambridgeshire jurisdiction. There is a wide main street with old cottages, old coaching inns and a church dating back to Norman times. The Haycock Hotel was once a private residence. In 1834 the young Princess Victoria, soon to become Queen, stayed here. In more recent times it was the home of Sir Bache Cunard, the founder of the Cunard shipping line. Walk past the church and turn right, down Bridge End. There are some lovely cottages along here too. Beyond the thatched one, on the right, you come to a signpost, pointing to a footpath across a field. This is the Nene Way. From the point where it reaches Wansford, back to Badby where it begins, is a distance of 70 miles. The Way was opened in 1990 by HRH the Duke of Gloucester and has proved a most popular long distance footpath. The County Council, the Countryside Commission and the countless volunteer fieldworkers are to be congratulated, for without their efforts, planning, finance and dedication the Nene Way would not have been possible.

The route back to Yarwell is now easy to follow. The footpath is well-trodden and every gate and stile has a Nene Way directional arrow disc nailed up. The route runs across the Nene meadows. There are plank bridges here and there, carrying the path across ditches, but nothing is difficult or arduous. Simply enjoy the landscape and the wildlife. There are marsh arrow grasses here, with bog pimpernels, ragged robin and other water-loving wild flowers. You may see herons and snipe; you will certainly see coots and moorhens. And in summer there are many species of butterfly to be identified. The footpath keeps mainly to the flat meadow land, with the rising slopes of arable fields to the right. Beyond a gravel track, which you cross half-way to Yarwell, other footpaths lead off to the left. These run down to Simsey Island and – further on – a weir sluice gate. Little detours can be made to these, time permitting.

Across the last field before Yarwell you aim diagonally towards the right hand end of a stone wall. There, a stile leads through to a path running between two walls (Yarwell manor house garden being over the one to your left). At the end of this you reach the road, where it bends sharply. Straight on would take you to the continuation of the Nene Way, as it heads towards Yarwell Mill. Turning right will take you back to the Angel public house.